ASTROLOGY

AND THE

INNER SELF

Also by Ray Douglas:

Dreams and the Inner Self
Palmistry and the Inner Self

ASTROLOGY

AND THE

INNER SELF

By

RAY DOUGLAS

First published in the USA in 2006 by Undiscovered Worlds Press
This edition published in the UK in 2009
by Dreamstairway

ISBN 978-1-907091-04-9

www.dreamstairway.co.uk

CONTENTS

Breaking the mould of traditional astrology

CHAPTER ONE

The Cycle of the Self

The aim of this book is to use the symbols of astrology to bring about a meeting between mind and soul; and having achieved *that* minor miracle, to help bring about a further encounter between soul and spirit. This in turn will precipitate a spiritual journey previously only to be dreamed about by saints, sages and seekers after truth: the hidden treasure that has been sought ever since human-measured time began. Why settle for less? Once the journey has begun, symbols will be of little further use. The inner self is more interested in realities.

If you follow astrology in the traditional way, to find out something about character and personality, and possibly to predict the ups and downs of fate, your calculations will need to be precise. If, however, you set out to use astrology to help you discover the inner self, and thence your own soul, your calculations will not need such precision. Why? Because the soul is broad enough to encompass both precision and imprecision. Paradoxically the inner self is greater than the outer personality, and the soul is greater than the inner self — potentially greater even than fate itself.

A horoscope is constructed upon the moment of birth, or coming into being, and as the moment at which a baby is born is seldom known or recorded precisely (and why, indeed, should it be?) it can be of no use to build a complicated edifice of precision upon the basis of a rough estimate. Even if the exact time is know for that crucial first breath, accurate calculations based upon it will work towards elaborating on the personality — on the *outer* self, moving further away from discovering the *inner* self, which has a collective basis. In my view, it is as well to be aware of this principle. Very few astrologers in the past have concerned themselves with the problem, and even fewer have cared to draw a line between the popular view of planetary *influence,* and the more subtle principle of planetary *synchronicity.* Dane Rudhyar, the French-American astrologer and musician who died in 1985, was a pioneer in this field. Though apparently not acquainted with the reality of his own inner dimension — his own soul — he was well aware of its existence, and he set out these matters very succinctly. His book *Astrology of Personality,* first published in 1936, formed my own introduction to the subject and moulded my understanding, such as it is, of astrology and its best uses. I hope that this book might carry his work a step further.

If you are fortunate enough to meet, or to have met with your own newly-awakened soul, and you are mature enough to realize that we all need spiritual guidance through life (not at all the same, you will note, as *religious* guidance), your journey is only just beginning. "Seek and ye shall find" is a piece of divine encouragement which works just as well after two thousand years. It doesn't matter who you are or where you look; it may be taken on any level. It works as well within the most devout, or the most academic spheres as it does in lowlier circles, or in the seamier side of life. It works as well no matter where we are looking from or where we seem to be looking to. The sincere seeker after truth may find the way whether the seeking is directed up or down, inwards or outwards, for the truth is already there, within the soul. Of course, it has been there all the time.

Certainly, the soul can be "born again" and thereby come to awareness. But exactly how it happens, the "mechanics" of it, will probably remain a mystery. There are always more ways than one to describe a mystery, divine or otherwise. Our brains are not made to encompass such matters, and sometimes we have to resort to the use of symbols in order to understand anything that seems to be non-material. Astrology, like algebra, is a system of symbols. Every occurrence, even if seemingly miraculous, is likely to have a material explanation — but that does not stop it being miraculous as far as we are concerned. So when we exclaim that some happy chance is a "miracle", we are not really denying the concrete causes of that event, or the natural laws of cause and effect, action and reaction. They will be operative too.

This is what happens when we seek an astrological explanation for our own existence, our course through this world. Events are liable to happen in tandem: the practical with the emotional, the logical with the miraculous, the material with the spiritual, and this fact illustrates the synchronistic nature of astrology. There is nothing special about astrology in this regard. It is merely a useful tool, a convenient area in which to "seek". When the time is right and the search sincere, the truth will be found and miracles will happen, for astrology is already present within the undiscovered soul, along with the cause of miracles, with faith and hope, love and hatred, despair and joy: all that is low as well as all that is high.

This book is not a standard work on astrology. Indeed, it may annoy some established astrologers by seeming to borrow, select and modify only those factors having significance for anyone seeking evidence of the existence of a personal soul. Such a search, if successful, will result in the meeting between soul and mind. Only then can the spiritual journey begin, for only the soul can experience spirituality. The inner self is the subtle aspect of the whole self, overriding the limitations of both the physical body and the surface personality. The soul, like a photographic plate, is sensitive to all events and influences, everything we experience, and records them. The soul, be assured, may acquire its own powers of speech, sight, hearing, and understanding, and will feel equally at home in divine and profane company. When we discover our own soul (being as yet bereft of *spirit*), it may not seem a particularly holy place. Indeed, at times it may seem like a garbage tip, because everything, high and low, has entered it to form its contents. There are two levels on which we can live — the material and the spiritual — and only the soul is familiar with both levels of being.

Yes, this meeting can certainly come about, and far more is involved than the mere possibility of contacting an exciting new dimension of "self". Quite literally, the possibilities are infinite. Look at it this way: the inner self is the seed of wholeness, placed at the moment of birth in the seedbed of the personal self. Representing the supreme being, the universe is the cosmic whole, filled equally with the smallest and the largest. The human microcosm reflects these cosmic parts coming together in an act of creation. When a child is born with an individual soul, a new cycle towards selfhood begins. Size and quantity are not issues of wholeness; these belong to the logic of materiality. The issue is one of *being,* coming into being, and it is "being" that has potential wholeness at each moment of creation.

Reality starts here and now!

We have to start from where we are; from what we are. Every moment is itself the synthesis of all past moments, and the source of all future moments. Synchronistic astrology logs the progress of fate, in general or in personal terms. We are reminded of the Buddhist doctrine of karma: "Whatever deeds a man may do ... they make a heritage for him". It is surely this mysterious heritage that militates against wholeness, against the completion of a whole cycle. Is it possible that by changing the synchronistic reflection of fate, we might be able to change fate itself?

This would be to set fate working against itself; to produce a state of inner tension. It cannot happen merely by wishing it; as with so many processes, a catalyst will be needed. Let us say that the journey of discovery can start only when some ray of influence from the outside penetrates the encompassing zodiac of fate — some kind of influence from some unknown source, somewhere "out there". Is this not the old, superstitious brand of astrology we have been striving to avoid? The myth of the tall dark stranger? Be assured it is not! There is indeed an influence which may reach us from beyond the influence of personality. It is not a personal influence, neither is it the arbitrary influence of uncaring gods, or planets: it is the non-personal influence of collective humanity.

Synchronistic astrology of the inner self is based upon the collective nature of mankind. Its propositions are essentially positive, creative, and realistic, leading the personality away from self aggrandizement, and equally away from self abnegation; the two extremes are equally negative. A negative attitude tries to analyse a situation, and tends to reduce any potential wholeness to its component parts so as to deal with them separately. A positive attitude, on the other hand, accepts the creativity of the moment, and expresses faith in the growth of wholeness — and wholeness is the province of the soul.

Soul-awakening is a necessary step towards achieving wholeness, and wholeness will certainly include the element of collectivity. The most helpful aspect of astrology is to point out the significance of what *is,* the quality of the moment, and moments collectively constitute the organizing principle of wholes. When the quality of wholeness pervades the moment, the possibility of becoming whole, the start of a new personal cycle, is brought to reality.

The cycle of wholeness must involve a recapitulation of the individual's past life in its entirety, and a conceptual return to its source: a return, that is, to purely human awareness, to the awareness that was always present in our very early childhood. From the moment of birth, the individual is unique and self-contained, yet compounded from elements that are common to humankind in particular, and the universe in general. The substance of our individual framework is essentially collective. Individual human nature in astrological terms could be said to comprise soul, earth and planets working together as a prospective whole.

All the life forms that we know can be said to have originated on the Earth, so as a symbol the Earth's motion could be said to represent physical life. This book is concerned with people, and we can take the Earth as a convenient symbol for mankind too.

In the dualism of the Earth's movement — firstly by spinning around its own axis, and secondly by the motion of its orbit around the Sun — we can see a duality of direction in life. The two types of movement may be taken to symbolize respectively the individual life, and the collective life of humanity. The Sun, by its gravity and its light and heat, is the source of earthly energy. To many religious people the Holy Spirit may be visualized as light. In both the spiritual and the scientific sense, light can be seen as the seed of wholeness, introducing the energy necessary for growth. Light, therefore, may be seen as a necessary condition of wholeness, and wholeness may be taken to imply the presence of light. All life is indeed a cycle, and it seems to follow that individual progress towards wholeness of the self must equally proceed in cycles, large or small, brief or protracted. Completion of the soul cycle brings light and life; unfulfilment equates to darkness and death. Fate and karma, if you differentiate between the two, are not necessarily evil, but they do represent the combined results of unfulfilled cycles, and in that regard they represent darkness. Conversely, the reconciliation of separated elements, the hoped-for state of wholeness, must be represented by light.

Fire, air, water and earth: following ancient tradition the four elements take their place in traditional astrology. The principle is to be found in various other systems of thought, to correspond with the four passions: "observing, desiring, striving and possessing"; or to the four moods: "sanguine, choleric, melancholic and phlegmatic". To the alchemists of old the four elements formed the basis of their research — popularly coarsened into a crude search for material wealth — hoping to find a catalyst, the philosopher's stone, that might allow the elements to flow together in mystical combination: To free the abstract psyche from the deadweight of the physical body, and "make gold from base metal" by forming a new spiritual seat of consciousness — the independent soul.

After a thousand years of utter confusion, alchemy evolved

into chemistry, and the original purpose was quite forgotten. But certainly the four elements or passions, as much now as then, need to be somehow combined if there is to be wholeness on the spiritual plane. As the Hindu Upanishads have it: "The elements of fire, air, water and earth find their peace in spirit. Spirit in the soul of man finds peace in universal spirit. Universal spirit rests in God". Synchronistic astrology attempts symbolically to combine the outer and inner, the physical and the spiritual sides of life, and makes plain the fact that, in their earthly cycle, they are in fact two sides of the same coin. The symbolism that we are using recognizes the "sameness" of all elements, whether material or abstract. A coin, after all, is valid only when both sides co-exist, though, in facing opposite directions, neither side may be aware of the existence of the other.

As a process, the cycle of fulfilment, which could becalled the attainment of wholeness, can never be defined by precise formulae. It may be recognized and shown in individual cases, for every case is unique to the individual. Its possibilities will always be indicated by a rhythm, a continuing vibration with high and low points; but it is not something that can be demonstrated or tailored to fit every case. It can only be seen as a whole.

Need astronomers and astrologers fall out?

Spirituality cannot be fragmented like materiality, neither can it be isolated, or personalized. It happens to the whole being at once, or not at all, and it is as well to remember this when studying astrology in this way. The more whole the perception, the clearer the truth, the brighter the inspiration to follow the vibrations of spirit. It is no use expecting planetary influence to assist the process; planetary movements can do no more than record the event. Synchronicity is the key. It is all too easy to regard traditional astrological interpretation as law, or to regard planetary interplay as some kind of judgment or arbitrary interference.

This has always been the point, too, at which astrologers and astronomers fall out, the latter seeing only scientific facts. There is the basic misconception engineered by the fact that the signs of the zodiac and the star constellations share the same names. But astrology, in the form familiar to us, is limited to our own solar system, and has no truck with constellations. And those distant stars in their turn can have no truck with our zodiac. Common sense still insists that the planets, equally with the stars, can have no influence whatsoever on human behaviour, or on the ups and downs of fate. The Sun and Moon may have some marginal effects of their own, but as far as Mars, Venus and the rest are concerned — nonsense!

So far, so good. Science has a material base; art has an abstract one, and I can see no reason for the two disciplines to quarrel. All life is rhythm. In our symbolism the rhythm of individual factors relates to the rotation of the Earth; the rhythm of collective factors relates to the Earth's orbital revolution. Nothing stands still. The universe is all movement, and serious astrology seeks to relate those cosmic movements which are closest to mankind with the movements of the life forces which manifest themselves, both in our oft-changing states of consciousness, and in the practical, material events which come to pass — in the form, in fact, of life itself. The larger the scale of outward rhythm, the more closely will it correspond with the inner self of the whole individual.

Perfect roundness, perfect wholeness, the circle — or rather, the sphere — is both the symbol and the reality of universal being. Every point is always turning towards the centre. Perfect universal beings *have to be* spheres. In the case of the planets, though themselves spherical, in astrological terms their sphere is their orbit, as seen from our earthly viewpoint. When casting a horoscope and assessing planetary relationships in a birth chart, this is an important factor to be considered.

If we take the Earth as a symbol of our own individuality,

as if it were the human body, its tides and its rhythms, its bodily functions and its moods, are certainly influenced to a greater of lesser degree by its satellite the Moon, and the Moon itself is totally dependent upon the Earth, as the sensations are dependent upon the body. In cosmic terms humanity is placed, it could be said, within the orbits of those planets which operate beyond our physical selves: Mars, Jupiter and Saturn, known to the ancients as the three gods of individual human aspiration; with the far more remote Uranus, Neptune and Pluto, discovered comparatively recently, seen by astrologers to represent the *collective* passions of humanity.

Bounded in their turn by the Earth's orbit are the orbits of Venus and Mercury, the god-symbols of emotion and thought. Our own orbit — our own self — encompasses these two alone. To be bound by the forces of emotion and thought, of heart and mind, which should be lesser spheres than our own, is to be bound by forces which are less than ourselves in their spiritual status. Astrology applied to the inner self makes it plain that individuals who are bound exclusively by these subordinate powers — by the heart and mind, or by the bodily sensations associated with the Moon, which is subordinate to the Earth — no matter how clever, how learned, how sensitive, how religious they may be, are necessarily less than truly human. Their potential is thwarted from the start.

It follows that the visible outer planets, Mars, Jupiter and Saturn, indicate the direction in which human aspiration should travel. The discovery of the remaining outlying planets with their yet more widely embracing orbits promised a yet higher destiny for the thoughtful astrologer aspiring to an inward state that could be said to be truly human.

Synchronistic astrology of the inner self acknowledges that all people, all beings are linked at a level which is deep as well as high. I personally see the zodiac as a smothering mantle of worldly desire holding humankind to the Earth, where they are limited by sensations, feelings and thoughts. The zodiac is indeed a symbol of all worldly passions, and it is itself represented as the bounds of a mandala — a universal symbol which is also a diagram of human potential. The kingdom of heaven is said to be within, and in the same vein a way through the encircling zodiac may be sought at the very centre of this personal and collective mandala — a point that touches all other points, and is central to every state of being. A circle may be large or small, and it may contain many eccentric circles within itself, but as a human symbol we all share the same central point.

Standard astrology can tell people a great deal about their own selves as individuals; but however valuable as an aid to understanding, an astrological birth chart cannot show the whole, completed self. It is necessarily embryonic, the seed which may or may not grow into a sturdy tree: little more than the scenic impressions at the very start of a journey. But although in the spiritual sense it can do no more than indicate possibilities, it does symbolize the nature of all possibilities open to that individual. In using symbols from a larger, macrocosmic scale to describe the microcosmic self, it will draw a picture of potential destiny, of individual *dharma,* but it cannot by itself tell us whether that *dharma* will ever be fulfilled.

An astrological chart, needless perhaps to say, can be interpreted only on the level at which the interpreter is considering it. One tends to perceive according to what one is. The coming to awareness and subsequent development of the inner self is dependent upon increasing wholeness, and wholeness cannot be perceived beyond the capacity of the observer. What can be perceived, however, by one seeking some kind of spiritual awakening, is past and present progress towards such an eventuality. Already, by having the patience to have read thus far, one has confirmed in oneself the state of receptivity that is essential for growth.

The type of receptivity that may lead to the possibility of

spiritual opening does not call for any particularly keen brain power, nor particularly sensitive emotions. At the conscious level: intuition, and at the unconscious level: instinct; these are the functions that can lead to the perception of living entities as wholes, and the ability to observe universal life patterns in operation. Instinctively, one senses the basic forces of the life cycle. Intuitively, one is able to experience them in reality.

Heart and mind, of course, must play their part. Revelations from astrological symbolism may be correctly perceived through the intuitive function, because this function above all others accepts symbols in their wholeness. But more than this is needed. Analysis of parts is a function of the intellect, whilst the evaluation of results is a function of the feelings. In the planning stage at least a certain co-operation between intuitive appraisal, emotional feeling, and analytical thinking, will be essential in arriving at a sense of *seeking* wholeness, however far from complete that search may seem to be.

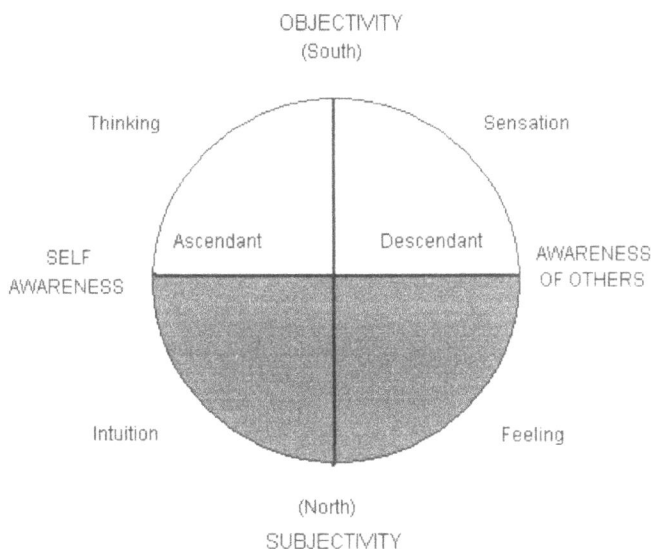

The birth chart : a personal mandala

A circle divided by a central cross into four segments, is traditionally used as a chart-symbol of the self — a personal mandala.The top of the chart is taken to represent the south-facing side, or daylight. The bottom of the circle represents the north-facing side, or darkness. The east is on the left, and the eastern extreme of the horizon is known as the ascendant. On the right of the diagram the western extremity is known as the descendant. This type of chart illustrates what is happening in the solar system at any known point in time and space, and may equally represent any event. In this case it represents the individual at the point of birth; the unique nature of that individual, and the fragmentation ensuing from an original state of wholeness. The horizon represents a line of awareness. The ascendant, at the rising of the Sun, is the seat of awareness of others. All planetary synchronicities or "influences" descending from above the horizon can be visualized as reaching us through the air; all those ascending from below the horizon can be thought of as reaching us through the Earth. The sum total represents the fruition respectively of the upper and lower hemispheres: conscious, objective and exterior; unconscious, subjective and interior. Above the horizon, therefore, all is objectivity, thoughts and sensations. Below, all is subjectivity, intuition and feelings.

The idea of potential wholeness was a preoccupation of the famous psychoanalyst Carl Gustav Jung, and his idea of four distinct psychological functions at work within each one of us was applied to the field of astrology in the 1930s by Dane Rudhyar. As involuntary human attitudes they may be symbolized by the four segments of the birth chart, to be summarized thus: the south-east quarter (top left on the chart) stands for thinking; the north-east quarter (bottom left) stands for intuition; the north-west quarter (bottom right) stands for emotional feeling; and the south-west quarter (top right) stands for bodily sensation. These divisions can indicate the channels through which cosmic awareness symbolized by the zodiac and the planets enter and exit the awareness of the inner self. In the language of symbolism, knowledge comes from the east, fulfilment occurs in the west. The spiritual power of regeneration in the form of intuition and the feelings, is said to come from the north; in the south by means of thoughts and sensations, this power can become crystallized as religion.

The re-creation of wholeness implies a return of the whole non-material self eventually to the spiritual source, as distinct from mere religious aspiration. As the Hindu Vedas put it: "Those who worship in public places and pride themselves on their piety and charity, travel to the south. It is the path that leads to their ancestors. Those who seek the inner spirit with steadfastness, faith and wisdom, travel to the north. It is the path that leads towards the ocean of life; towards the land of immortality".

As time goes by the rhythm of life in general seems to become more and more materialistically orientated; but by this very fact the idea of spirituality as an individual movement towards psychic wholeness, stands out and becomes more readily definable. It is good that we should experience materiality to the full normal extent, for this too is part of the nature of "wholeness". The depths of materiality are balanced out proportionately by the rarer heights of spirituality. We could not really experience the one without the other. A fair balance is essential.

Personal time — collective space

It is of course the Earth's revolution on its own axis that creates the ever-rolling horizon with its own fixed point of reference — the Pole Star. Taken to represent each human individual, during the course of one single revolution the Earth is bathed as it were in all the possibilities for change that are available to it, facing each planet and each sign of the zodiac in turn. One can consider it as a clock face in motion. The single hand of this clock is the horizon between ascendant and descendant — sunrise and sunset. From an individual viewpoint the hand of this clock is stationary whilst the dial itself revolves in a clockwise direction, recording time and logging the spinning of the Earth. From a broader viewpoint, the ascendant-tipped hand itself could be said to revolve in the

19

opposing, anticlockwise direction, as the horizon continually changes in relation to the constantly rising Sun.

In a completed birth chart, the zodiacal position of the Sun will indicate the exact *position,* within the Earth's orbit, of the individual's birth. The cross, symbol of life on Earth, in determining the position of the ascendant and the descendant, the zenith and the nadir, will represent the exact *time* when the birth took place — the degree reached by the Earth's rotation around its own axis.

Astrology has often been accused of lacking logic, and this is largely true, more particularly perhaps with our selective brand of astrology, intended to be relevant not so much to personality as to the inner self. Rudhyar called astrology the "mathematics of wholeness", because, where logic deals with separate parts in *space,* astrology deals with wholes in *time.* Logic functions by taking this and that fact and fitting them together, perhaps making use of mathematical symbols in doing so. Astrology, on the other hand, considers the whole pattern of astrological symbols, and that symbolic wholeness is taken to represent the physical whole. This is a bringing together of time and space, with time as the symbol, and space as the subject of the birth chart. Within the space-time continuum, if time is subordinate to space, the individual must be subordinate to the zodiac.

Synchronistic astrology is essentially "do-it-yourself", because in order to be really useful everything about the subject should ideally be known and recalled. When the birth chart is calculated a new quality and a new dimension is added — the quality of time. Space symbolizes the individual's ancestral structure, his or her human status, ethnic background, physical appearance. Time, on the other hand, symbolizes personal content, individual potentiality. The ancestry of space, it seems, gives rise to the potential wholeness of time. But this is not the whole truth: if it were, it would imply that the personality (the most individual and perhaps therefore the most subjective dimension of humankind) symbolized by the Earth's turning on its axis, carries the most significance for spiritual development. Wholeness in the spiritual sense implies a broad relationship with the "collective experience", subtle and often hidden from the conscious mind. It is both movements taken together — time and motion in space — that will record outward expansion, the rising of the inner self. It is important to distinguish between a turning inward on oneself by use of the will as a method of "inner development", and the collective way of submission to real influences from beyond the zodiac, indicating the way back to the source.

There is a third motion of the Earth — the Great Polar Cycle — which in astrology symbolizes a periodic influx of cosmic creative powers. In scientific terms, I dare say, the wavering Great Polar Cycle and the resultant precession of the equinoxes is caused by the continuous gravitational effect of Sun and Moon on the Earth's spinning equator. The cycle is said to take 25,868 years to complete, and during this period the "fixed" north point will have changed as the polar axis of the Earth points in turn towards different stars. The nature of incoming cosmic powers, and thence the potential for world spirituality, is said to change as the Earth enters each successive era — now, and for the next two thousand years, the Age of Aquarius.

In astrological terms, the north pole is considered to be the point at which cosmic magnetic energies enter, symbolizing the power of divine consciousness. The opposing south pole is the point of departure for these forces in a modified form: the *yin* of Mother Earth receiving spiritual influences from the bright *yang* of divine awareness. In this respect the Earth as a planetary whole, has often been said to represent the "planetary individual" — a Buddha-like figure whose head is haloed by the aurora borealis. But this type of "wholeness" is not appropriate for the human individual; such a person would have become crystallized in individual selfhood. Such a person would still be bound by that vast web of materiality symbolized by the zodiac. The whole self must include the non-self with the self: truly spiritual wholeness must include all planetary orbits, as the collective experience, within its own being.

In practical terms, individual contents are constantly undergoing change and modification in their relationship with the collective. Only the foundation for the self — the "space" of the birth chart — remains unchanged and unchanging. Time is indicative of change, the continual interplay of influences which surround the individual, changes which are aptly symbolized by the ever-changing zodiac degree, and the ceaseless movements of the planets, seen and unseen.

Meaningful events may seem personal to you and me, but we represent the microcosm, and symbolically such events are registered on the vast meter of the macrocosm. Having recognized this, and having established the link between personal experiences and the workings of our solar system, having studied the resultant patterns as they applied to the past, we can make suppositions for the future, because astrology is a discipline of symbols. The art of putting astrology into practice consists in the use of cosmic symbols as an aid to understanding. To argue whether cosmic patterns can or cannot have influence over human affairs is to misunderstand both the practice and the purpose of this art.

The human recipient of spiritual influence is the soul: not some theoretical principle, but the human soul in reality. Within the solar system the planet Earth represents a kind of prison for the soul, and the perimeter of that prison is the zodiac. In order to escape this prison, the soul must gain an introduction to the spirit which alone can provide access to greater worlds beyond. It is helpful meanwhile if the mind can first gain an introduction to soul. Any astrological doodler may find that *inner* significance may best be charted not on a personal plane by precise calculations involving the Moon and inner planets, but on the collective scale through the zodiac degree and the more easily plotted, widely orbiting outer planets.

Precision applied on the personal plane can only lead ever more deeply into the thrall of karma and an unfulfilled cycle. The life of the inner self is lived not on the personal but on the collective plane, for the "inner" is indeed greater than the everyday "outer" self. Using astrology to help uncover this fact is essentially a do-it-yourself art, once the seed of the idea has been sown. An individual as the native of a birth chart, sits at the centre of a personal universe, and all else is symbolized as revolving around this unique point in time and space. The most creatively constructive interpretation may be made by the subject alone, for the individual self is its foundation.

CHAPTER 2

The nature of the zodiac

In the previous chapter I said that the Earth, in the language of symbols, represents the human self. The zodiac then must be seen as the human environment, the world of the Earth; the personality, the cultural inheritance, of the Earth. On the birth chart the zodiac is to be taken as a series of points of reference which serve to plot the positions of Sun, Moon and planets in relation to the orbital motion of the Earth. I have come to see the zodiac as a living, vibrating mantle of energy, a patchwork quilt of life forces, a force-field which surrounds the Earth and controls or constrains the lives of its inhabitants, plant, animal and human. From the point of view of spirit, in respect of the Earth, the zodiac must represent no less than the bounds of materiality.

But what exactly is the zodiac, in sensible terms, if not simply that remote background of stars? It provides fixed references for each of the 360 degrees which custom has ascribed to any circle, so is it merely a convenient name, or series of names, for the path of the ecliptic, the track along which our Sun *seems* to move? That certainly is the usual definition of "zodiac" — the "animal belt". The line between symbolism and factuality becomes blurred when I say that the zodiac is indeed a spiritual matrix through which our planet must spin. In the astrology of the inner self, in the cycle of becoming, of potential wholeness, the zodiac must be taken to represent a sheltering cocoon of life forces, interwoven, vibrating in harmony, regulating natural instincts, bestowing human personality.

Many people, even a few astrologers, have been misled by the nominal link between the zodiac and the constellations which supplied the familiar names of the twelve signs. As everyone now knows, the grouping of a constellation into its familiar shape is little more than an optical illusion formed by quite unrelated stars many light years apart. From a rational point of view of course it is true that the zodiac is simply the Earth's orbit. But within this orbit, it is equally true to say, is contained all that is possible for all creatures on Earth, including humankind: within the zodiac is the potentiality for selfhood, and the possibility of that selfhood coming to completion.

I have said that the zodiac is a spiritual matrix. But if its function is to bind materiality around the Earth, it would seem to follow that it must stand in opposition to true spirituality. The two extremes seem forever at odds. But without materiality no creature could function or live. Our human bodies are solidly material; our very thoughts are products of our material brains. It is very plain that, whatever our spiritual aspirations, materiality is something that we could in no wise do without.

With this quality of materiality still in mind, the zodiac could be said to represent the substance of all life forms on Earth, and the familiar signs of the zodiac represent twelve distinct but basic types of life substance. Applied to human personality, the simplest analysis will show that within each basic type exist numerous subtle variations. There are no "good signs" or "bad signs", as far as people and their birth dates are concerned. Both the highest and the lowest of qualities may be found in any one of them.

Reiterated daily by popular astrologers, the traditional characteristics ascribed to each sign are well enough known. Although no fixed level of being, no moral or spiritual status, can be attributed to them, they do indicate basic personality traits in individuals, both human and animal, that fall under their sway. Remember that the zodiac represents a cycle of degrees, beginning for convenience with the northern spring equinox. Each degree (and in more general terms each set of thirty degrees, each twelfth part of the whole) builds upon the preceding signs or degrees and reinforces them, justifies their characteristics, and carries their principles a stage further in every case. It will do no harm to restate their basic qualities in terms of human development:

Aries
carries with it the abstract idea of the egoistic self, the first realization of individuality, the sense of "I am" that, in its fully developed form, distinguishes humans from beasts. It exemplifies the will to *be,* to commence new growth.

Taurus
represents the developing substance of abstract Arien desire, a gathering of material evidence to the self. This sign inherits the basic idea and solidifies it in a tangible way.

Gemini
synthesizes the relationship between the previous two, self and substance. It integrates and digests these two basic modes of expression and projects them outwards, communicating them in understandable terms.

Cancer
again returns to new realizations, new individual beginnings; but being now in possession of both the expression and the synthesis, has the power to commence practical growth rather than merely to will it.

Leo
is all concrete expression, symbolizing solidly real projection of the principle of personal growth, with creative activity to confirm and strengthen individuality.

Virgo
brings discrimination and judgment to bear on the enthusiastic projection of selfhood. It considers the results of those past actions and modifies them in the present with the power of reason.

Libra
instinctively makes peace, acknowledging more fully than the previous types the rights and needs of others. It rejects the selfishness of "I am" and seeks to unite differences.

Scorpio
represents the substance of the Libran balancing instinct, seeking to unite with others in wholly practical terms. It represents a renewal of self-centredness, in terms of *feeling*.

Sagittarius
conjoins the qualities of Libra and Scorpio, and expands them outside of itself through the urge to understand and experience new and more complicated relationships.

Capricorn
tames the Sagittarian spirit of expansion and builds a firmer foundation for outside relationships, expressing an instinctive longing for a human society of permanence and stability.

Aquarius
expresses these ideals of permanence in new emotional and creative ways, feeling a need for experimentation into the possibility of broader relationships and new modes of conduct.

Pisces
represents the process of weighing, summarizing and judging of all past ideals, discriminating, meditating inwardly upon outward qualities, and setting the pattern for a new personal cycle to begin.

When superimposed on the individual mandala, the zodiac begins to show something of the qualities that clothe and embellish the naked soul, as well as the primitive aspects of character that may lurk beneath the acquisitions of civilization. One needs to look beneath, around and above superficialities, both of personality and of inherited cultural attitudes, to discover the innerself — the subtle self which alone can contact soul, and which alone can hope to receive influences finer than those ascribed to the zodiac.

The elements

Fire, air, water and earth — each sign of the zodiac is said traditionally to possess the nature of one or other of these fabled elements. The idea is often expressed in somewhat simplistic terms, for instance, *fire:* the Arien personality is forceful and persistent; *water:* the Cancerian is emotional and deep; *air:* the Geminian is characterized by his restless thoughts; *earth:* the Taurean is down to earth and reliable.

But these similarities are coincidental. There is a far more subtle and diffused significance which can be attached to these four elements as they form part of the zodiac. As we are taking the zodiac itself to represent the web of instincts and the pattern of natural lifestyles here on Earth, rather than seeing the elements as passions that rule the individual, it will suit our special purpose better if we equate them with the "passions" that rule Earth itself — nature's life forces, as they
affect humankind.

Our basic humanity, the inbuilt program that determines our biological characteristics, has already been determined before birth. Personality is largely inherited by way of our genes, but the instincts which can be said govern our specifically human behaviour and which I call the passions, have to be acquired from outside the physical body, via the instinctive level of consciousness. It is these instincts that can be described as embodying the quality of the four zodiacal elements: fire, air, water and earth.

It is no use thinking of these elements as possessing a stable quality, or occupying a known level of being. It will become plain that they each contain an unknown number of grades, or ascending cycles. Take "fire", for instance: there is smouldering fire, which can safely be held in the fingers; then there is raging fire which can form towering infernos capable of devouring steel and concrete. There is light earth, fine enough to trickle through the fingers; then there is hard clay and solid rock, and even molten metal deep within the Earth. Each quality of life force is a blend of these elements with an intelligence uniquely its own. Within this abstract blanket of cosmic elements, filling Earth's life forms under the general name of "instinct", there are the animal life forces, which provide the drive, in one, to behave and feed like a lion; in another, to behave and feed like an antelope; in another, like a snake. As animals are unrooted and free to roam, one can see that these animal life forces will be strongly akin to the element of air, although fire, water and earth will also play a part.

Animals are limited to animal instincts, plants to plant instincts, minerals to the instincts of materiality. But because of our unique nature, poised, it has been said, halfway between heaven and hell, between the abstract realms of spirituality and the gravitational pull of materiality, humans are not limited to human instincts. Since leaving the pristine state of Eden with its purely human, purely instinctive way of life, our search for the benefits of materiality have filled us with all the instincts, all the passions of nature, and we cannot now escape their influence.

The animal life forces direct the lifestyle and movements of the giant blue whale as surely as they direct those of the microbe. They are responsible for social order in the teeming life of insects with their million-fold variety; with the shoaling of fish, and the amazing migratory capacities of birds. These instinctual life forces bestow energy and strength, arrogance and selfishness, forcing creatures under their sway to experience the joys of triumph and the sorrows of defeat. They lead the hounds to outrun the fox, and equally they lead the fox to outwit the hounds. Thus they are constantly in a state of tension within themselves; but they are at one with the Earth, for they ensure an even balance of populations and resources.

Plants function on their own brand of instinct to exactly the same extent as the animals. No plant can think its way through life from the seed to the forest mould. The plant life forces or instincts bestowing the urge to behave like an oak tree, or a nettle, a cactus, or a vine, may seem on first consideration to be serene and gentle. But on further consideration it will soon become plain that they are no such thing. Frequently it is the fate of plants to exist in hostile environments. They are bound to the earth by their roots, apart from tiny life forms able to float freely in the air or sea currents, and they cannot choose the place where they live. A plant must be ruthlessly competitive if it is to survive beyond the seedling stage. The life forces appropriate to them ensure that, if they cannot adapt themselves to the opposition of other plants, they must either overcome that opposition or succumb to it.

Animals usually have a sense of family, or group, or species, and may look after their own in various ways; but with plants there is no such consideration. The welfare of neighbouring plants — even siblings from the same pod or clones from the same branch — is of no account; their rule of life is "number one". In astrological terms, we can say that these plant instincts will have a special relationship with the element of water, which soaks into the earth and gives life to thirsty roots, though the other elements too must play a part.

Through ceaseless internal strife, these fierce and selfish plant instincts balance themselves out over many generations, and lead to the creation of closely-knit plant communitiesable to function individually by inter-relating habits: roots feeding at differing depths, foliage seeking sunlight at differing heights. The numerous species provide for their own survival by means of incredibly varied modes of reproduction. Every unit seems to co-operate with the whole. But when an apparently peaceful plant community is disturbed, whichever plant happens to find itself temporarily advantaged wastes no time in taking over as much territory as it can, suppressing other plants in its path. The "peaceful" woodland community evolves only through the "passion" of ruthless selfishness.

To be identified with the abstract element of "earth", the material life forces can be said to provide a physical impulse for the behaviour of atoms and all the particles which make up the Earth, or indeed the whole material universe, regulating the form and density of solids, gases, minerals and metals. They are perhaps the least subtle of these nebulous life forces. They are certainly the coarsest and probably the most powerful, and nothing material could exist without them. They constitute the mechanics of gravity and magnetism, controlling the tendency of matter to accumulate or disperse.

All these basic instincts will exist quite separately from the creatures which they motivate. A creature can lose its appropriate animal instincts if isolated from its proper environment for too long, cut off from the source. But it will never lose the basic physical instinct of continued existence. Fire, air, water and earth in their abstract sense must coexist in all life forms, but the wholly material "earth" will be the most pervasive and persistent. Humans, animals and plants are all material objects on Earth, and all are physically motivated by material energy.

Mutable		**FIRE**
Fixed	HUMAN INSTINCTS	AIR WATER
Cardinal		EARTH
Mutable		FIRE
Fixed	ANIMAL INSTINCTS	**AIR** WATER
Cardinal		EARTH
Mutable		FIRE
Fixed	PLANT INSTINCTS	AIR **WATER**
Cardinal		EARTH
Mutable		FIRE
Fixed	MATERIAL INSTINCTS	AIR WATER
Cardinal		**EARTH**

31

Civilization, nature and intuition

Fate has decreed that we as humans must imbibe a share of all the "lower forces". It is no bad thing, for they provide the wherewithal of civilization: instincts prompted by materiality may bestow greed, but they also bestow the ability to make and use tools, to build houses, to make and wear clothes. All these things are certainly part of the divine bounty for people on Earth, but as they represent the lowest force, the subtle force of materiality within the zodiac, they cannot be intended to form our psychic centre of gravity. They are far less than "human" in nature. As Hindu tradition has it: "There are three great powers in nature, created to govern the minerals, the plants and the animals. When the soul of man is governed also by these powers, he strays blindly along the paths of illusion, wandering endlessly from death to death". Any creature governed by nature is automatically governed by the Earthly cycle of birth and death, and this really is the very bones of the great spiritual search, the possibility of transcending nature, of breaking free from the seemingly endless cycle of reincarnation involving the inevitable death of our passionate lower human soul. Finding a way to make this great escape is the whole purpose of our brand of astrology. The greatest problem with our attempts to shed these natural bonds is the fact that these passions are not *bad*. It is not as though we are merely seeking to resist temptation or anything so simple. These life forces have become really necessary to our lives.

Plant forces for instance certainly introduce the passion of ruthless arrogance into the human psyche, but they also instil the need for competition, for striving in the face of opposition, for putting in an effort to improve our lives. They are finer forces than the material, and they too are useful for the development of civilizations. But, like the material instincts themselves, as part of the laws of nature, they cannot be intended to dominate human actions; they too are far less than the truly "human". The animal forces in their turn bestow pride and clannish behaviour, and often a seemingly insatiable appetite for sex. They are of a still finer

THE NATURE OF THE ZODIAC

nature than the others, and we cannot escape imbibing them. The very air we breathe is said to be full of minute organisms, both animal and vegetable, so there is a continual interflow of instinctual matter between human, animal, and plant. The animal forces too have their uses in human development, for without their instinctual drive there could well be no sense of culture, no urge to build nations, no determination to achieve one's ambitions. And, of course, they too are part of nature's laws over which we as humans *ought* to remain spiritually aloof.

Finer than the animal forces of the zodiac, fine enough indeed to permeate the web of the zodiac through its densest layers, are the instinctual forces actually intended for humans alone. These, expressed intuitively, give us the ability to judge, to observe, to discriminate, to do all those things that set us apart from the animals. It has been said that people at the time of Abraham were truly "human", being less influenced by the "lower" life forces. For reasons we shall soon discover, compassion was unknown to them. Their hearts and minds were not as active as are the hearts and minds of modern people, and they had yet to experience the competitive spirit of territorial acquisition, or the tenacity to manufacture and build. I am identifying this human life force with the astrological element of "fire". All the elements need to be present in all living beings, but fire, we might say, is the fire of life, and only humans are able to make proper use of fire.

The Descent of Mankind

The spiritual history of mankind is usually thought of as a slow climb from an animal-like or apelike state, through primitive stages of nature worship and sun worship to an ever more sophisticated understanding of one almighty loving God. This is the historical view, but it does not represent the spiritual reality of the situation. The reality of it can perhaps be best understood in terms of these life forces operative via the zodiac. If we plot a sequence in these terms it seems to confirm a quite opposite view: that our collective worldly advancement has been in a direction *away* from our high origins, and *down* into the depths of materiality. The spiritual direction of evolution has been away from the source, away from God, away from human childhood to the materiality of adulthood, coincident with the adult's capacity to think keenly and feel deeply. It would seem, in other words, that people cannot be truly adult, that civilization, arts and sciences cannot develop, until we have *grown out of being spiritually human;* until we have descended among the lower orders and become adulterated by them.

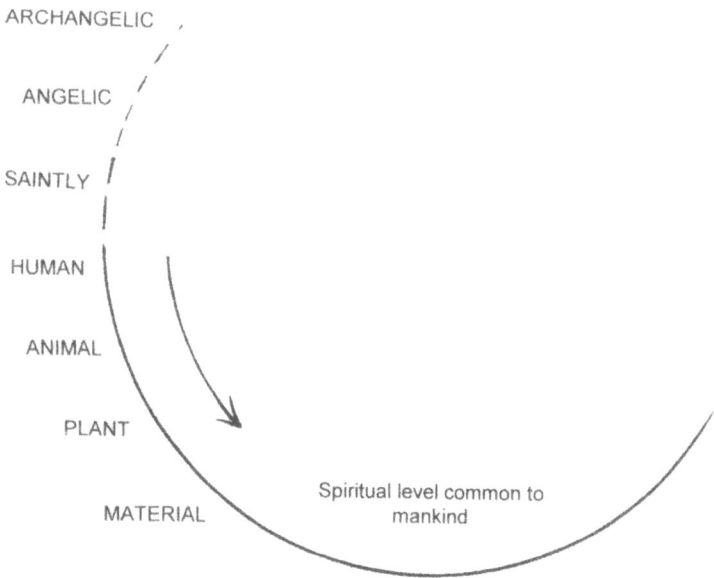

ARCHANGELIC

ANGELIC

SAINTLY

HUMAN

ANIMAL

PLANT

MATERIAL

Spiritual level common to mankind

The Descent of Mankind

Nowadays, it is very clear, we humans have become thoroughly adulterated and filled with what are really subhuman instincts — in this sense, immersed in nature. But all is not lost. With the development of heart and mind, provided mind does not become too domineeringly powerful, may grow the capacity of intuition, and the intuitive realization that the positive qualities of striving, thinking and learning (that is, "the passions") are precisely the cause of this human descent. The hoped-for meeting of mind and soul, and the subsequent search for wholeness, for reunion with the source, cannot really be conducted with these instruments. The understanding must arise spontaneously that this particular journey needs to follow the direction of *human instinct,* an all but forgotten function that comes into operation only when the gross passions of "wanting" are stilled. The will — the everyday functioning of heart and mind — cannot be used for this noble purpose.

Another quote from the Upanishads: "Lacking spirit, the soul of man that governs body and mind is itself governed by the forces of nature ... By itself, soul is powerless to repudiate alien forces and seek such as are proper to the lives of men". Elemental life forces stand in the way of possible contact with spirit through the medium of soul, and those elemental forces cannot be put out of action by means of the will, since the will is subordinate to them and governed by them. Expressed somewhat differently, the direction of mental development is downwards, towards the centre of materiality. The insulating layer of the zodiac covers the Earth. The way to escape the zodiac therefore cannot be "downwards" by strengthening the mind, but upwards and outwards by way of the truly human instinct, through the oppressing passions, to and beyond the soul to the realm of spirit.

Because they do not *think,* creatures below the human level seem barely influenced by life forces which do not concern them. They follow only their own level of instinct. All flesh is grass, it is true, and all physical forms are material objects. But each life form has its own instinctual course and adheres to it. It is only when *we* take a hand and transmit *our* passions, that instincts may seem to have become adulterated. The pet dog, for example, influenced by human company, may begin to behave as though filled with the plant passion of competition, or the material obsession with possessions. The ability of humans to act as "channels" for forces both higher and lower than our own true nature is often unsuspected, and is a point to be touched on later.

It may not be out of place to stress that "spirituality" is not at all the same as "religion". Religious leaders are often described in popular terms as "spiritual leaders" when plainly they are no such thing. This is not to say that religion and spirituality cannot function together, though religion is often a matter of cultural background, and little more therefore than an accident of birth. Essentially, spirituality is a matter for the soul, being filled with spirit. Religion is a matter for the heart, the symbolic human heart, the seat of emotion whose feelings may be noble or base. According to the biblical Prophet Jeremiah: "The heart is deceitful above all things and desperately wicked".

Passion, in the Christian sense, means "suffering", but this is not what we usually mean by "passion", in the sense of vehemence or intensity. Suffering may be found at all levels of being, but there are no vehement "passions" in the spiritual ethos. "Passions" are to be found in religion, along with fanaticism, because they reside in the heart. Both are of this Earth, and cannot approach the Almighty, cannot encompass spirit. You may feel something strongly, but this does not make it true. Truth is to be found in the reality of experience. There has always been an unfortunate tendency among emotional and often pious people to suppose that strong feeling strengthens truth, or that the "passions" equate with truth.

Realization, through intuition, may creep up on one. There may come a distinct moment of change in the lives of religious people, a change of direction. In one of his sonnets John Donne wrote "I am a little world made cunningly of elements, and an angelic sprite". This angelic sprite may be behind it all. How else can we make contact with the centre of being, with the seat of human instinct, with the blank sheet of the inner self that receives all influences and can respond, not with the elements, not with passion, but with wisdom: the spontaneous awakening of the soul?

The cycle of the zodiac

In the first place, we should understand that our position in the zodiac is not limited, whatever our Sun sign or the rising degree of our ascendant. Governed by nature, human life follows the full cycle of nature — that is, the full cycle of the zodiac with all its possibilities. We can follow this in ways suited to our own cultural expectations. Our familiar system of astrology originated in the northern hemisphere. Nearer the equator and in the south people have evolved somewhat different systems. The northern seasons are distinct, and it is easy to see why the zodiac cycle, though continuous, is said by Europeans and North Americans to begin with the season of new growth, the spring equinox.

By experiencing seasonal rebirth every year, the Earth can be said to symbolize the collective life of humanity as it progresses from birth to death. From new birth, the human individual should progress through the spring-like flush of youth into the full bloom of summer, to ripen and mature during the autumn, finally reaching the winter of old age and death. In this sense the life of the Earth represents the whole of human life in each orbit of the Sun.

The whole process can be summarised in tabular form, presenting a sequence that should be recognisable in anyone's life. The table that follows summarizes the steadily changing progress of a maturing individual. This is the background familiar to the soul; though normally unfamiliar to the mind, it is the canvas upon which each life is painted. It shows how the driving instinct and the dominant passion changes as we become older, a subtle background that will show through the personality in a way adapted to the cultural background of the individual. The sequence is not affected by birth sign or ascendant degree. Those factors are always present, of course, and each newly formed personality will be moulded and stamped accordingly. But in the broader, cosmic view — essential when seeking soul and thereby spirit — all births can be said to take place at the spring equinox, the birth-point of the Earth. Every developing soul then has to grow through each of the zodiac signs in turn, progressively absorbing fresh characteristics as it grows.

ASTROLOGY AND THE INNER SELF

AGE	SIGN	ORIENT.	PREOCCUPATION	QUALITY	DEGREE
0-7	ARIES	outward	urgent projection	Awakening	0°
				watching	15°
7-14	TAURUS	inward	productive security	feeling	30°
				enjoyment	45°
14-21	GEMINI	outward	adaptive variability	desire	60°
				striving	75°
21-28	CANCER	inward	defensive protection	daring	90°
				sincerity	105°
28-35	LEO	outward	authoritative power	conviction	120°
				explanation	135°
35-42	VIRGO	inward	critical analysis	invention	150°
				experimentation	165°
42-49	LIBRA	outward	harmonious unity	rumination	180°
				discovery	195°
49-56	SCORPIO	inward	intense penetration	memory	210°
				valuation	225°
56-63	SAGITTARIUS	outward	extensive exploration	discernment	240°
				freedom	255°
63-70	CAPRICORN	inward	prudent discipline	wonder	270°
				dependence	285°
70-77	AQUARIUS	outward	unconventionality	conservation	300°
				anticipation	315°
77-84	PISCES	inward	unworldliness	hope	330°
				reassurance	345°
					360°

38

All this, it should be stressed, takes place quite irrespective of individuality symbolized by the actual birth sign, logged by the Sun in space and the ascendant in time; irrespective, that is, of environment, fate, karma, heredity, or outside influence. Beginning with Aries the twelve zodiac signs, each a twelfth part of the Earth's orbit, are traversed by the self, taking seven years to log the thirty degrees of each. By this reckoning, to complete the cycle of nature, the ideal human life span would be seven times twelve, or eighty-four years. This, by tradition, is termed the "Lifespan of the Patriarch" or, equally, the "Matriarch". By the age of eighty-four, whether he or she realizes it or not, a person will have lived through the whole range of human characteristics, sampling every possibility open to them within the limits of their own individual capacity.

One can recognize the rhythmic changes in outlook that take place in oneself, if only by remembering how it was for you at some previous date. The characteristics attributed to each sign of the zodiac are well enough known, and overlaid on these, it becomes easy to see how the changing signs fit into the life pattern of any developing individual.

As the table shows, every sign of the zodiac is regarded either as "inward-looking" or "outward-looking". The unconscious habit of looking inwards or outwards in one's approach to life — the introversion-extraversion factor — really does alternate, not only through adjacent zodiac "birth" signs, but also in 7-year cycles throughout an individual life. It indicates the changing outlook that any normal person experiences as they go through life. On this factor depends whether people look for causes within or outside of themselves, and it has significance for the progress of the awakened soul, too.

Most of us occasionally look back at our own lives. There were the formative infant years, when everything was urgent and immediate, and instantly expressed. At this stage the mental processes are only just awakening, and the feelings are projected outward. Then from the age of three or four, and still within the sign of Aries, comes the natural urge to "watch", to learn about life. Arien adults are not baby-like, of course, although there is perhaps a childlike sense of urgency about them. The breadth of the symbol should be respected. All life forms must experience their own specific version of the sequence. It would theoretically be possible to plotthe inner progress through the zodiac cycle of any creature, elephant or starfish. From the viewpoint of nature, human progress is only potentially "human" in the spiritual sense.

At seven years of age the individual experiences a change of sign. From this time on comes an intensely sensual period of exploration, a greedy eagerness, as it were, to sample every new flavour or sensation. Later, this drive broadens and becomes more physical, developing into a search for active enjoyment around the age of ten and into the early teens. This is an inward-looking search: "How do *I* like this? How does that affect *me*?" This is the Taurean principle!

At around fourteen years children start looking outwards again. Their most urgent need seems to be the necessity of fitting in with their peers. Their desires are insatiable, and they really feel the need for someone outside of themselves to share their feelings with. This is a time too when youngsters branch out determinedly into all the activities open to them, in a spirit of adventure that soon develops into the competitive striving of young adulthood. These are typical Geminians, entering the difficult but exciting period of adaptation to maturity, their experiences pulling them first one way and then another. Though individually they are seldom aware of "soul", all this is soul activity, functioning irrespective of outside influences.

Next comes the Cancerian period lasting from the age of twenty-one until twenty-eight, the period of "daring", when young adults are very much centred in personal feeling whilst they venture boldly into the unknown: an age for the pioneer. "Sincerity" becomes a way of life, though probably unformulated as such. But with this sincerity may grow a sense of guilt for all the various influences that have been entering the soul, unsuspected since childhood and only now making their nature known. Approaching the age of twenty-eight, we are fortunate if we can "make a ladder of our faults" and use them as a means for growth.

The onset of the span of Leo is often explosive and always unexpected. The latter part of this 7-year span may be deeply concerned with a search for enlightenment. The fruit of previous sincerity is an open acknowledgment of all shortcomings. There may take place an honest reassess-ment of one's situation, followed by the wish to create a more significant, more authoritative position in the world. This is often the most confident period of one's life.

The span of Virgo is the fruition of all experiences to date, resulting in an attitude that contrasts sharply with that of the ebullient, confident Leo. This is the time for the discovery of principles greater than anything hitherto known, a quest for influences finer than any normally supplied by the world. Frequently this is the time when contact with the "great life force" becomes a reality. If so, it becomes a period of intense spiritual experience.

The span of Libra signals a more adventurous phase when having received the best of available influences by way of the quietened, receptive soul, the individual quite involuntarily again turns outwards. The result this time is to bring the spiritual fruits of the ruminative phase to meet and mingle with the coarser influences of the world round about. The next seven years, typically, will be a time of intense physical activity, coupled with sensitive feelings.

At the age of forty-nine, the individual may quite suddenly tire of feeling like an emotional island in a sea of physical activity. It is time to become *outwardly* emotional whilst inwardly receiving finer influences that will give food for thought. On entering this phase of recollection and reassessment, the imaginative capacities will flourish as never before. Sexual impulses too will seem to grow from within, without necessarily finding a smooth outflow. Scorpio is very much orientated towards a sexual mode of expression!

The span of Sagittarius often brings with it a state of confusion. The individual will have been feeling a powerful need to look outwards, to broaden all experiences, physical, emotional, mental and intuitional. It is a time for adventuring with caution, examining new possibilities with care, and this time a suitable vehicle for expression is sought and probably found. It is the time of life when many people find their true forte, when their natural gifts and latent talents can be developed to the full.

Capricorn heralds a new span of gathering together, reassembling, and putting to good and profitable use. From the previously undisciplined application of newly discovered talents, a new and more controlled lifestyle can now be organized. Deep inside, the individual often senses peace, filled with an unexplained sense of gratitude.

Now, as the cycle of nature draws close to its completion, the symbolism of the outlying planets grows in importance as these collective factors grow in strength. From the age of seventy, the span of Aquarius signals an excellent time for quiet inward submission to a higher possibility — the collective   soul   of humankind. If the Capricornian span brought about the possibility of reconciliation with Saturn, with the inevitability of death, this Aquarian span symbolizes the individual's ability to pass safely through this barrier, to leave heavier passions behind, and to experience the strange "collective passions" symbolized by Uranus, co-ruler of Aquarius.

Finally the ageing individual looks inwards once again, submitting to finer impulses from the inner self — impulses which, in astrological terms, may actually be capable of penetrating the

Saturnian rings of death. As a symbol of the individual soul, the ruling planet of Pisces is Jupiter; but it is co-ruled by Neptune, symbol of the collective soul itself. This is the Piscean span that completes the whole eighty-four year lifespan, and as it draws to a close it embraces an increasingly unworldly sense of reassurance and peace.

Many people can see these changes very clearly in their own lives, up to whatever age they have reached. The cycle has been one of nature within the confines of the zodiac, but it has been operative by way of the soul. The closer a person is to his or her own soul, the clearer will the progression seem. When the soul is wide awake, it will be very clear indeed. Each change of perception during the cycle has its own distinctive flavour, like a vivid memory of times long past. Each change may have been instantaneous, even violent or brutal, occurring perhaps in a flash of inspiration; or it may have been gradual and barely perceptible. At all events, one usually gains the impression that life has somehow shifted gear. Each 7-year phase is in fact a barrier; a hurdle to crossed, and with some, the experience can bring with it an excitingly new understanding of the meaning of life.

Not everyone of course is fated to complete the Lifespan of the Patriarch, or Matriarch. It is certainly not a condition for advancement. It simply logs the birth, death and rebirth of the Earth in its orbit through the seasons. It is merely a chronometer, recording the progress of nature. But it does form a background which is common to all, and it is helpful to locate oneself within this cycle and from there to choose a promising time to contact the great life force, once the possibility of this encounter is known and understood.

CHAPTER 3

Earth and the threefold cycle

In the first chapter the mandala of the birth chart was described as having four quarters which can each be related to one of the basic psychological functions, thought, feeling, sensation and intuition. These functions are not normally marked on the chart, but their location and the roles they play should not be forgotten when they seemingly disappear, to be replaced by the so-called dial of mundane houses.

When one speaks of "mundane houses", or "mundane astrology", one is using the word not in its sense of "unadventurous" or "uninspiring" but in the sense of "Earth", relating to the influence and affairs of the world. The Earth in its annual cycle, as we have seen, can symbolize the individual human life considered apart from any outside influences. In this sense, mundane astrology transfers itself to personal astrology and must feature strongly in this highly selective study, our astrology of the inner self.

The twelve mundane houses, or psychological divisions, can be considered in various ways; but however they are interpreted, they are always taken to represent twelve distinct but smoothly sequential compartments of basic awareness, common to all humanity. Against this apparently fixed background the personal horoscope is plotted, an essentially human dimension to be considered when plotting the pattern of the zodiac and planets at any given time. As a basic framework common to everyone, it represents the psychic groundwork; the dwelling place of soul (as distinct from "spirit").

The dial of mundane houses could be seen as a tract of virgin land which may be cultivated into a beautiful garden, or allowed to erode into worthless desert. From a rather more romantic viewpoint, it could be said to represent the Garden of Eden before the temptations of the encircling serpent of the zodiac introduced the polarities of good and bad into developing hearts and minds, and scattered humanity along different paths. It can certainly prove a useful aid in distinguishing between those human traits that are innate, and those which have been introduced through outside influence.

The point of individual birth on the personal chart is the dawning horizon recorded by the ascendant degree, corresponding with the soul's entry into the first house. If we think of the ascendant as a moving finger, the "point of self", we can see that it moves through life in an anti-clockwise direction as it passes through each house in turn. During its course it should plot the growth of personal understanding, the young child's increasing awareness of its own physical selfhood.

Each cusp or dividing line between houses, as it is passed in turn by the point of self, carries with it a certainly quality of ascendancy. It becomes, as it were, the eastern horizon anew, bringing a new day pregnant with possibilities in the light of a new guiding principle. This is before the zodiac degree, the Sun, the Moon, or the planets are even taken into account. The cusps therefore represent a kind of ladder of significances or critical stages, or varying modes of creative possibilities. The very fact that they represent a renewal of soul fabric grants the individual a certain reprieve from the consequences of former attitudes. It is at the cusps that a person becomes able to expand and change.

Houses whose cusps occur on the ascendant, the descendant, the zenith and the nadir of a birth chart are referred to as "angular houses" (numbers 1, 4, 7 and 10). They carry the sense of projection, the putting into action of a newly discovered function. The so-called "succedent houses" (numbers 2,

45

5, 8 and 11) signify a reaction to the actions expressed through the angular houses. These reactions may be positive or negative, and if the latter they can imply that the inherited weight of materialism has tended to smother the possibility of truly spiritual selfhood. The so-called "cadent houses" (numbers 3, 6, 9 and 12) are said to make manifest the results: the sum, or the fruits, of the preceding two houses.

The Dial of Houses

New meanings, or a new set of principles — and again these may be either positive or negative — may arise whenever a new level of selfhood is reached. The principle of successive subtle changes is operative whenever earthly life cycles are involved, on whatever level they are being considered. They are all subject to the zodiac, and bearing in mind what has already been said about the nature of the zodiac, it is inevitable that the mundane houses share to a certain extent the characteristics of the zodiac signs.

Thus, the first house represents self concern, like that of a newborn infant, and corresponds with Aries. The second house represents possessiveness, like a child discovering the possibilities of having things and actually owning them, and is typified by Taurus. The third house symbolizes the adaptability necessary when seeking a relationship with one's environment, one's place in the world, as expressed by Gemini.

Together, these three houses are governed by intuition — the driving force of a young child, and a function at once higher and lower than either thinking or emotional feeling. Lower because, related to instinct, it is experienced in common with the beasts, and higher because it is a particular function of the soul, which alone is able to gain contact with celestial life forces higher than the human.

The next three houses are governed by the emotional feelings, and in the fourth house these reflect domesticity as expressed by Cancer; in the fifth house they reflect the Leonine brand of creativity; and in the sixth house they relate to one's manner of personal expression, typified by Virgo.

The third set of three houses in this cycle is governed by the physical body and its sensations, and when these three are traversed by the point of self they inevitably represent a time in one's life of increased physical activity.

Included   are   the   seventh   house,   concerning   Libran diplomacy and personal relationships, the eighth house where the Scorpionic preoccupation is with sexual regen-eration, and the ninth house, featuring the physical projection of Sagittarius, charting a conscious adjustment of one's attitude to others in the light of all past experiences.

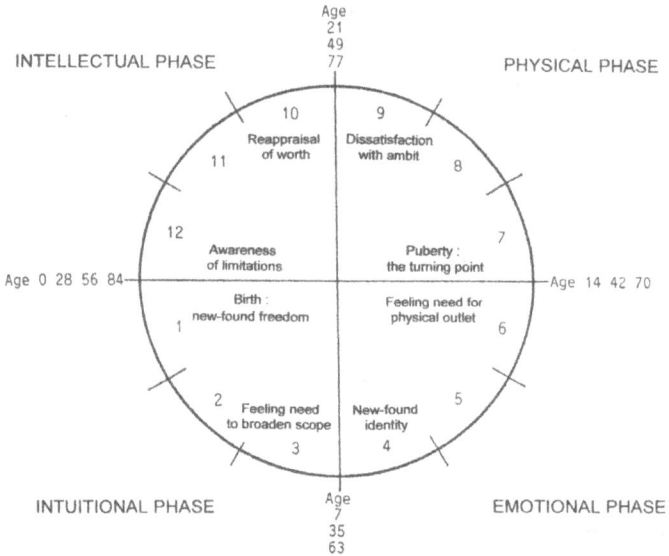

The Threefold Cycle of Houses

The final three houses are governed by the thinking function: in the tenth house concerning the putting into practice of one's newly adjusted relationship with society, as typified by Capricorn; in the eleventh house regarding the manipulation of one's position within that society, as typified by Aquarius; and finally in the twelfth house, as a synthesis of all that has gone before, and reflecting the inner conflict so typical of Pisces, comes the often painful reappraisal of one's place in the world.

We have already seen how the horizon on the chart can be considered as the hand of a clock, measuring personal progress; and we have seen in the last chapter how an individual soul, in the guise of Earth itself, progresses through the seasons of the zodiac. Now we can consider a further set of cycles, based on these "houses of the soul". Each moment has its creative potential. By setting out to understand the nature of one's own personal cycles we aim to identify the points in time when a new creative cycle can begin; to this end we should think in terms of movement.

In everyday life a householder might feel the need to move to a new area, to a better house, a more congenial district. The soul too, having reached the end of a cycle and having moved from house to house — or maybe only from room to room within the same building — finally feels the urge to seek broader horizons. Such a move may involve something of an upheaval in one's way of life; it will be an adventurous step to take, abandoning the comforting routine of the old milieu.

Progress seldom comes from looking round for reassurance, meaningful progress may well involve some element of risk, and unforeseen problems; the choice belongs to the individual. But there are differing levels of attainment, and even when the best available choice has been made, the general trend of "progress" may seem to be on a spiritually downward curve leading towards a hardening of materiality. But it may nevertheless still work towards the development of the whole self.

The threefold cycle of houses is a convenient way of expressing the collective progress of the personal soul, and the instinctive attitudes and reactions associated with this progress. It carries a stage further the 84-year Lifespan of the Patriarch, or Matriarch, and the three consecutive life cycles are closely identified with the principle of "past, present and future". It is not, of course, the only way of analyzing personal progress, but it is a particularly convenient one — a cycle within a cycle, a wheel within a wheel.

As the point of self passes in turn through the four separate functions — intuition, feeling, sensation, thinking — each house is "occupied" in turn for two and one third years, during three consecutive revolutions of twenty-eight years each. In the course of an 84-year lifetime, twenty-one years will have been spent under the dominant driving force of each basic function.

The threefold cycle can equally well represent the upward spiral that we ought to follow, if the soul comes to its own awareness and the awareness of mind, and if we are able to live our lives in a way orientated towards spiritual attainment. In the majority of individuals, selfhood becomes so embroiled with the lower life forces of nature represented by the zodiac, that we remain set, as it were, within a recurrence of the lowest cycle. And even when the completed spiral is attained, its level in astrological terms may remain within the orbits of the inner planets: limited, that is, by thoughts and emotions. Only through an inward rejection of "passions" — quite involuntarily as far as the mind is concerned — can the truly human instinct take over and set the individual on an upward course. This is the integrating principle symbolized by the Sun having been imbibed by the inner self.

Compare this idea with the diagram of planetary orbits in Chapter 6. During the first twenty-eight years of life one's inner spiral can reach no higher than the orbit of Mars. During the second 28-year cycle one's orbit should include not only Mars and the lower planets, but also Jupiter, the god-ruler of the lower soul, reaching to the limits of the time god, Saturn. In this sense one can become greater than Zeus, chief of the ancient gods. The third 28-year cycle in this spiral, when successfully accomplished, will allow the inner self to pass the Saturnian rings of death and take up residence, as it were, within the "collective" orbits of the outer planets. There, one can hope for the final rebirth, the symbolic passage through the zodiac, beyond our remote overseer Pluto, now to be considered as the custodian of materiality itself.

Body, soul and spirit

These three cycles have been called, respectively: "the ancestral" (that is, of the past); "the individual" (of the present); and "the collective" (of the future). They reflect, firstly, those characters which were inherited; secondly, the action or use that is being made of that inheritance; and, thirdly, the outcome resulting from these factors. From our present viewpoint, a more appropriate name for these three would be: the cycle of body; the cycle of soul; and the cycle of spirit.

The first cycle is concerned chiefly with our vessel for life on Earth. During childhood and young adulthood our personal and physical needs are of prime importance for each one of us. These comprise our orientation and beliefs, and our ethical guide will be our family and the traditions of our own native culture, the moral and religious restraints and obligations that we happen to have inherited. On its completion, this cycle represents the fulfilment of all that is past in relation to one individual life. In effect the whole cycle of that life, with all its available possibilities, will have been lived out in just twenty-eight years — but on a personal and ancestral level only. On its completion it must start again, but this time, if all goes well, it will be lived on a more exalted level.

The second passage through the dial of houses we call the soul cycle, not because it applies more particularly to the inner self than does the preceding cycle, but because the human soul comprises the whole contents of a person, and not merely the inherited parts. This time the characteristics which are being stirred within are of a deeper nature. Cultural tradition may be important, but it should not be allowed to override personal development; its days in command should be numbered when a person's twenty-eighth birthday arrives. The soul itself should now be the leader, and a person's entry into the first house of the second cycle should herald the awakening of inner awareness, the first stage of spiritual consciousness. To put it another way, rather than a ready-made set of rules, morals and beliefs, a person's guide from the age of twenty-eight onwards should be their entire psychic content, even if that should comprise the bad as well as the good.

The third and final revolution of this great spiral, reached when a person has passed the age of fifty-six, is named the cycle of spirit. If they have not already done so, it is time now for influences from beyond materiality to infiltrate the smothering layers of the zodiac. As the product and culmination of the two previous cycles, this time the mundane houses are occupied with an eye to the future. A person's guidance should now come, via the soul, from beyond both the self and the ancestors. The older person's ethical guide may be seen as "collective experience", or the spiritual principle, or even the Holy Spirit, depending upon the destiny of the individual.

Let us examine each cycle in greater detail. During the first seven years of life a child lives largely by intuition, gradually becoming more and more self-conscious as an individual, but still under the spell of subjectivity. There is little differentiation as yet between external facts, and mere ideas; objects are not really solid. During the passage through the third house at around five or six years, the child begins to relate more surely to his or her environment. Purely "human" instincts become gradually left behind, but the psyche remains emotionally as well as physically dependent and wholly subjective in judgment.

At about seven years, the embryonic emotions which have been incubating for the past few years begin to take over from child-intuition as the driving force. The possessive infantile phase broadens out now into a new individual identity. In nine and ten year olds, adventurous creativity is the norm. At twelve or thirteen the ego begins to crystallize into true selfhood, and rebellious self-expression tends to replace dependence on home and family.

The newly-found ego leads outwards into the beginnings of true objectivity. Sexual also desires begin to develop, and the accompanying crisis can be severe. Often, it is a time of physical illness brought on by the shock of transition from a safe world of the feelings to a new and aggressively physical environment, with no experience of handling it. For the first time, the outside world is seen through truly objective eyes, and its apprehension may cause a ripple of fear. There can be few teenagers who do not experience an acute awareness of an imperative need to adjust to the rapidly changing conditions during this period, emotionally as well as physically, and with this new awareness an often perplexing degree of self doubt.

By the age of twenty-one personal and physical relationships will have been well tested, and modified by a growing awareness of the needs and natures of others. While still strongly influenced by parental influence, the psyche reaches its majority in the light of social experience accrued during the previous seven years, the period during which the child has been growing into adulthood.

Now follows the burden of social responsibility that accompanies initiation into adult society, and the age of twenty-five or twenty-six usually sees a conflict of identity. A crossroads is reached, with no clear signpost, only a pressing choice that must be made, relating to loyalties, behaviour, customs and company. It can be a time of great anguish, and if the individual is liable through karmic content to suffer from depression, this is when its worst effects may be felt. Such a one may well feel hampered by social or moral restraints or taboos that seem to run contrary to his or her own instinctive nature.

Inherited characteristics may be a matter of genes. More mysterious, perhaps, is the accumulation of personal karma which seems to enter the vessel of the soul at the moment of birth – an additional inheritance that has lain trapped, as it were, between onion-skin layers of the inner self, demanding release. This deeply interesting subject may be approached through a study of the individual birth chart in its relationship with the zodiac degree symbols described in the ensuing chapter. The awakening of soul to consciousness sees the commencement of a process entailing systematic removal of these inhibiting karmic factors — a process which, by way of synchronicity, may perhaps be logged by the outlying planets.

HOUSE	FUNCTION	AGE	FIRST CYCLE
1 Arien selfhood		1	Functioning purely on human instinct
		2	Growing awareness of material things
		3	Steady development of emotional feelings
2 Taurean possessiveness	INTUITION	4	Growth of thinking capacity
		5	Exclusively subjective modes of thought
		6	Realization of fully dependent selfhood
3 Geminian adaptability		7	Constructing relationships with others
4 Cancerian domesticity		8	Emotional feelings succeeding intuition
		9	Increasingly objective modes of thought
		10	Strengthening the sense of "self"
5 Leonine creativity	FEELINGS	11	Growing appeal of external experiences
		12	Experiencing need to reduce dependence
		13	Striving to acquire physical expression
6 Virgoan analysis		14	Experiencing physical attraction to others
7 Libran diplomacy		15	New physical modes of expression
		16	Past feelings put into physical practice
		17	Sexual sensations take on new urgency
8 Scorpionic intensity	SENSATIONS	18	Desire to form equal relationships
		19	New defensive independence
		20	Uncertainty about future course of action
9 Sagittarian projection		21	Apprehension about future relationships
10 Capricornian conformity		22	Tendency to feel aggressively defensive
		23	Experiencing need to use intellect more
		24	Reappraisal of past and present values
11 Aquarian manipulation	THINKING	25	Tendency to feel depressed or gloomy
		26	Feeling dissatisfaction with old methods
		27	Aware of moral and social shortcomings
12 Piscean conflict		28	Feeling need for a new approach to life

Inner tension

The more "individual" a person's character, the more strongly he or she takes after the birth-ascendant sign. The "collective" aspect of personality, on the other hand, most strongly reflects the Sun sign. Indeed, some astrologers and others interested in the subject are able to tell, from physical characteristics alone, whether a person is centred mainly in collectivity, or individuality. The ascendant type

EARTH AND THE THREEFOLD CYCLE

HOUSE	FUNCTION	AGE SECOND CYCLE
1 Arien selfhood		29 Impact of new intuitional realizations
		30 Relief from depressive undercurrent
		31 Abandonment of inherited advice
2 Taurean possessiveness	INTUITION	32 Feeling need to satisfy natural instincts
		33 Powerful desire to live for the present
		34 Seeking uninhibted satisfaction
3 Geminian adaptability		35 Belief in the rightness of free thought
4 Cancerian domesticity		36 Seeking new emotional satisfaction
		37 Departure from recent selfish habits
		38 Feeling that life has switched direction
5 Leonine creativity	FEELINGS	39 Experiencing a new identity
		40 Experiencing new inner creativity
		41 Developing soul-based inner culture
6 Virgoan analysis		42 Sense of higher status and self-approval
7 Libran diplomacy		43 Feeling need for more independence
		44 Energetic physical needs given priority
		45 Physical application given to old ideas
8 Scorpionic intensity	SENSATIONS	46 Hard work dedicated to efficient results
		47 Changes of occupation and orientation
		48 Difficulty adjecting to new lifestyle
9 Sagittarian projection		49 need for significant new venture
10 Capricornian conformity		50 Tailing-off of physical enthusiasm
		51 Dramatic change of work orientation
		52 New intellectual aspiration
11 Aquarian manipulation	THINKING	53 Past experience put to intelligent use
		54 New associations and circle of influence
		55 Frustration at personal limitations
12 Piscean conflict		56 Awareness of need for further change

of personality, as a rule, becomes most easily identifiable soon after the age of thirty-five, as the emotionally-felt "new-found identity" grows out of the intuitional phase that preceded it.

When the individual makes contact with the "collective soul" and its "collective passions", a great tension can be set up between these two "selves", characterized by the Sun sign and the ascendant. When both are of a like nature (referring to the four

HOUSE	FUNCTION	AGE	THIRD CYCLE
1 Arian selfhood		57	Period of uncertainty losing past beliefs
		58	Unusual ideas arrive to give new hope
		59	New insights into familiar problems
2 Taurean possessiveness	INTUITION	60	New plans are made for the future
		61	Building new foundations for the future
		62	Concern with preparations for security
3 Geminian adaptability		63	Feeling a new direction has been forged
4 Cancerian domesticity		64	A new phase of heightened awareness
		65	New understanding of past uncertainties
		66	New value judgments about current trends
5 Leonine creativity	FEELINGS	67	New awareness of innermost feelings
		68	Reconciled to inevitable aging process
		69	Feeling need to work for posterity
6 Virgoan analysis		70	Seeking more practical achievements
7 Libran diplomacy		71	New set of pressing priorities
		72	Practical realities overrule preferences
		73	Physical shortcomings become insistent
8 Scorpionic intensity	SENSATIONS	74	Experiencing new rhythm of life
		75	Physical frustrations and critical moods
		76	Adjustments to lifestyle broadening outlook
9 Sagittarian projection		77	Quiet search for meaningful pursuits
10 Capricornian conformity		78	Surge of ideas bringing new solutions
		79	Practical arrangements removing worries
		80	Delegation of responsibilities
11 Aquarian manipulation	THINKING	81	Growing understanding of own psychology
		82	Apprehension about physical problems
		83	New challenging ideas, or old memories
12 Piscean conflict		84	Growing sense of peaceful acceptance

elements, fire, air, water and earth) the tension is less. When the two signs are distinctly opposite in character, tension can reach crisis point, sometimes bursting out in odd behaviour or "unsocial attitudes". This itself constitutes an inheritance over which the individual can have had no control.

Cyclic rebirth through the mundane houses is a time of great significance. If the inspiration is not accepted and followed, the frustrated psyche, unwilling to face the ordeal of impending cyclic rebirth, may choose to remain within the symbolic womb of becoming, and languish on the level of ancestral culture. But if all goes well, symbolic rebirth means that the individual becomes free to leave his or inherited,regulated past, and concentrate instead on building a solidly individual present.

As children, inwardly passing through the first three houses of the first cycle, we were still in touch with our own souls, though to a progressively decreasing extent. With the growth of emotional feelings, the contact was finally lost. From then on, our hearts and minds took over control of our lives, with all their ups and downs. Typically, the late twenties are somewhat turbulent times psychologically. As the first cycle comes to a close our minds can seem in a helpless whirl. But then comes the first rebirth and the start of the second cycle at the age of twenty-eight, and quite suddenly, sometimes instantaneously, a new intuitive grasp of our life situation arrives to provide whatever answers we need; and with this new understanding, often enough, comes freedom from the old, stifling, conventional restraints.

Provided the second cycle has "taken" satisfactorily, once this soul cycle has been established, we may find we have regained soul-contact by means of a new intuitive driving force. A person approaching thirty should be living largely by intuition, "following instinct", and this artless faculty can provide the urge to look deeper into the inner self. Through becoming aware of a mysterious capacity we did not possess before, we may well have caught a glimpse of new and still more mysterious worlds open to exploration. With this renewal typically comes a longing for contact with true spirituality. Instinctively, the individual must seek such a contact, and seek it urgently.

Of course, the flash of intuition that served to realign our progress was not the result of our own wisdom. It was an automatic and perfectly natural function of our own inner nature; a straightforward cyclic rebirth, re-entering the first house. It is only as we approach the close of our second intuitional phase, towards the age of thirty-five, that we will begin to entertain doubts about the wisdom of continuing our intuitive course through life, correct though we know it to have been. It will be an emotional time. Now that our intuitional capacity has developed as far as it is able, it is the turn of our feelings to be dissatisfied. All this happens quite automatically. We come to realize that a new way of expressing ourselves is needed; a new emotional identity; a new kind of creativity within our lives.

By the time we reach the sixth house at around the age of forty, we should have established that new basically emotional identity — or rather it will have established itself — rising out of our own intuitional understanding and expressing itself in terms of feeling. A new and more subtle ego will have emerged from within our own personality, and the concern of this ego is not the body, but the soul — the sum total of all our past experiences, physical, emotional, intuitional and intellectual.

Once again, if our lives have been forming a spiral of development, we will grow increasingly dissatisfied. Our milieu has not been substantial enough; our achievements have not been noteworthy enough; our degree of independence too slight. We begin to search for a more physical, more practical, more challenging outlet. Forty-two is the classic age for "changing horses in mid-stream", and the discontent we feel can often bring real hardship with it. When our habits become set, it is not easy to adopt a new pattern of life, particularly when this must involve a severing of ties, increased independence and an unexplained need to face the unknown future alone. In effect it amounts to a new puberty, and as with actual puberty there is an obsessive need to fit in and make a success of whatever looms ahead — the next step towards achieving true maturity.

The seven-year itch

It does not apply only to shaky marriages: the seven-year itch is more than a figment of the imagination. Perhaps it was more clearly to be seen in days gone by: for instance, John Wesley used to claim that he burnt all his sermons every seven years, realizing that his perceptions would have changed over that period.

Continuing our journey through the mundane houses of life, as another seven years pass and we approach the age of forty-nine, discontent creeps in once again, and we are liable to feel that our routine lacks the intellectual qualities, the mental stimulation that we need. We are facing yet another traumatic period of reorientation. Our friends may remark that we seem to be throwing away all that we have built up over the past years. independence alone, it seems, is no longer enough. A new understanding has been growing inside us, filling us with ambitious thoughts of our own potential value to society as a whole.

Up to this point, perhaps, we have assumed that our future was assured. Now we come to see that it is not. All our building so far had been for the present, the here and now. We had never really considered the future. It occurs to us very forcibly that there is a great deal of building still to be done; the idea of "building for posterity" may well cross our mind. We will probably have been working very hard over the last seven years; but how about our own soul — have we forgotten about that? We are obliged to experience a period of anguish as we reassess all that we are and know.

The reason for all this disturbance, of course, will be the fast-approaching point of possible rebirth, the possibility of slotting into the next cycle. If all goes well, at the age of fifty-six we will once again be touched and subsequently guided by a new intuitional understanding; a new grasp of our situation in life. We will not be boasting when we say that our wisdom has been growing and leading us along sound lines during the past seven years. Our intellect has brought us to the present, but it is only now, under the reawakened guidance of intuition, that we can really begin to plan for the future.

Many people at this stage in life give careful thought to planning for the future security of their dependants, foreseeing possible eventualities. Some may concentrate their efforts as well on producing some special work by which the world may remember them. A few perceive intuitively that the time has come to build a spiritual future for themselves — and by doing so ensure that their dependants' welfare is taken care of in a way undreamed of by the materialistic majority.

At the age of sixty-three the emotional function again comes to the fore, strengthened this time by the recently acquired intuitive understanding. With this revitalization of the feelings comes a quite different sense of selfhood — a new ego again, but this time on a collective scale. This is not the selfish "me" of the twenty-eight year old, nor the more subtle "soul-ego" of the forty year old. This is the focal point of a much broader personality, orientated towards a far larger concept of life, embracing hopes of immortality.

Though we call it the spirit cycle, many people in their third cycle of life may not seem at all concerned with matters of the spirit. But although this aspect may not have come to their awareness, they can still lead highly significant lives. At around sixty-five they will have become reconciled to the inevitability of death, and found a way to use their emotional centre of gravity as the practical basis for a valuable phase of creativity. At retirement age, one is often free to concentrate on pleasant tasks and interests that one never had time for previously.

This refreshing mood may continue through the sixth house; but before long it is liable to give way to a premonition of crises to come. The symbolic third puberty at seventy years is inevitably a time for major readjustment, as emotions give way to a brooding sense of frustration. The physical body becomes increasingly querulous, as one's habitual approach to daily events and tasks no longer works as well as it once did.

If this stage of inner and outer reorientation is weathered successfully, at seventy-seven an individual enters the intellectual phase for the final time. Many great thinkers have reached the height of their powers during this seven year span, between seventy-seven and eighty-four. Physical shortcomings may be almost forgotten in the excitement of new understanding.

People in the twelfth house for the third time will be only too well aware that their current situation cannot last long; that a major reorientation is due. But the successful completion of the full cycle of houses at the age of eighty-four has brought with it a wealth of supportive wisdom and serenity — serenity which will carry them safely across the mysterious final barrier.

CHAPTER 4

The zodiac degrees

Seeing the universe as we do from a continually changing series of viewpoints which we call the zodiac, subjectively we tend to take a geocentric view, although objectively we know the solar system to be heliocentric. From whichever viewpoint, the degrees of the zodiac will still symbolize our own rhythmic relationship with the Sun and with the universe as a whole.

As far as humans on Earth are concerned, both time and space can be clocked and measured by the endless band of the zodiac. The meeting point of time and space can be recorded by the zodiac degree, each degree a fleeting focus for the ever-changing pattern of life forces. As the projection of time into space, one degree represents the distance travelled through space during one complete revolution of the Earth, the amount of space covered in a day and a night. With each of its successive revolutions, the whole face of the Earth is bathed in the flavour of that degree, that particular instinctual blend of influences. As the product of both axial rotation and orbital revolution, as the integrator of these two, the individual and the collective, each degree of the zodiac has to be a powerful symbol of personal creative growth.

The zodiac degree can be taken as the point at which any individual life enters the life of the planet, and in this case it implies too the stamp of individuality on the collective character. Like any other event occurring within the focus of a particular degree, the birth of an individual can be said to receive the distinctive stamp of that degree, retained for life — but this is not to imply that the event was in any way isolated in time or space; it is not exclusive. Through the spinning of the Earth, during which the whole of the zodiac faces the whole of its surface, each degree can be said to include within itself the whole cycle of seasons, and all the varied conditions of Earth, human, animal, vegetable and mineral. It contains within itself, as it were, an imprint of all the remaining three hundred and fifty-nine degrees of the zodiac.

As we have seen, the dial of houses could be taken as a personal reflection of the surrounding zodiac, the photographic plate over which the image of each changing degree must pass. And so, in collective terms, the 360° cycle of the zodiac represents a natural progression for humankind. Representing a day and a night, the sequence may be divided into twenty-four hours or "spans" of 15° each, corresponding with the dominant principles governing the developing personality (see the table on page 38).

If the dial of houses can be said to represent the soul, and the zodiac its contents or substance, the zodiac degree represents the quality of those contents, and the quantity of that "substance" absorbed by the individual during that time. In personalizing the instinctual energy which is behind all life, it records the development of selfhood, and expresses the possibility of progress in either a materially orientated direction, or a spiritually orientated one.

You will see that, within each span, the first five degrees form the first "step" representing the instinctive level of being. The second step of five degrees represents the emotional level; the third step of five degrees represents the mental or intellectual level. This symbolic stairway in space could be visualized as the route by way of which natural evolution takes place. In inner as in outer space there is no real "up" or "down"; from the common sense point of view, one's progress from birth to death, from 1° to 360°, is wholly an ascent. From the viewpoint of potential spiritual attainment, however, forward progress constitutes first a descent, followed later by an ascent.

Characteristics of the various Zodiac degrees can perhaps

best be appreciated through the use of pictorially descriptive symbols. Word-pictures such as these can seldom be taken literally; they should be considered as useful catalysts in the process of interpretation. Periodically they have been brought up to date in their imagery by means of the intuitive function. They may reveal the potentiality of whatever is considered in relation to their degree, not as a matter of factual accuracy, but of value. Many astrologers limit their use to "mundane astrology" relating to places and things, but this, in my view, is incredibly short-sighted. They each carry an implication of significant content, an extra dimension as an inspirational aid to understanding. This is synchronicity at work.

A comparison may be made with dream analysis. When offered for possible interpretation dreams often exhibit the remarkable capacity to take a form that will be familiar, not to the dreamer but to the interpreter. A Jungian-minded analyst, for instance, will be told about "Jungian" dreams; a Freudian-minded analyst about "Freudian" ones. This is in the nature of living symbols, because it is in the nature of the collective unconscious and the inner feelings which present its images in the form of dreams. That which I call the collective intelligence can oversee the process of presenting symbols appropriate to the moment. As the degree symbols originate intuitively as symbols of awareness, they too are able to reveal "meanings", often more reliably than intellectual analysis could achieve.

Inevitably, our instincts have become overruled by the pace and complications of modern life. A quiet study of the degree symbols and their structural rhythms, in combination with our own birth chart, may help us as individuals to arrive at the spiritual point we might have reached naturally by following those instincts without the hampering preconceptions inseparable from civilization. The following section suggests how these symbols can be understood in terms of personal character, and the changing moods of the moment. They may just as well be applied to any situation or non-personal event.

Astrologers are familiar with the "Sabian" label, often applied to these and other similar sets of symbols. The set of symbols given here is a direct descendant of the set updated for 1920s America by the astrologer and dramatist Marc Edmund Jones, and dwelled upon at length by Dane Rudhyar in the 1930s. To quote Marc Jones they are "catalytics to the astrologer's higher understanding, the development of which will enable him to add content and implication to every factor of life". And to quote Dane Rudhyar, they "can be related to one of several ... levels of consciousness. Hence the application of symbols to individual cases requires a technique based upon the higher understanding". Unscientific they certainly are, and to coax astrology away from the unrelenting precisions of science towards the flexibility of intuition is, in my view, to nudge it in the right direction.

When using the degree symbols, remember that the degrees themselves are given as whole and ordinal, referring, that is to the duration of the first degree, the second, third, and so on. Thus, a reading of 23°10' falls within the 24th degree, and the symbol that will apply is 24°; *Fresh air blows into a room, stirring the curtains.* With regard to the personal sign of the ascendant, each degree takes an average four minutes to pass over the horizon. With regard to the collective sign of the Sun, the 15° "hour" represents a full span of approximately fifteen days, with each degree covering more or less a whole earth-day.

In terms of human cyclic development, remember that the zodiac, in representing a cycle of degrees or steps, can be seen as a ladder or stairway of psychic progress. Each degree — or in more general terms each set of 30 degrees, each a twelfth part of the whole — builds upon the preceding signs or degrees and reinforces them, justifies them, and carries their principle a stage further in every case.

ARIES

AWAKENING — FIRST STEP

1° *A woman emerges from the primeval sea*
Confident, enthusiastic, affectionate, reasonable , not given to self-doubt, optimistic, active, eager for new experiences. Not usually religious but aware of spiritual potential. Not immoral, but tends towards innocent amorality.

2° *A man laughs and jokes with his friends*
Friendly, outgoing, reacts strongly to outside influences. Essentially a sociable person who needs friends. Keen observer of human nature. Likes to feel in charge of fate. True to principles. Cloaks mishaps with humour and tends to frivolity.

3° *The map of a country resembles a man's face*
Highly principled, with respect for established tradition and morality, but forward-looking and often in conflict with convention. Feels urge to explore cultural differences. Possesses a strongly intellectual appreciation of beauty.

4° *A boy and girl walk hand in hand through the woods*
Happy, confident person, self sufficient, extraverted, physical, sensual. Casual in approach to social relationships. Understands opposite sex well. Short tempered. Appreciates importance of principles, but often ignores them.

5° *A white and yellow triangle in the sky*
The power of reason tends to be valued above the inner feelings. One who enjoys spreading new ideas. Can seem intolerant of the less talented, and careless of others' feelings. Prefers abstract pondering to practical application.

ARIES

AWAKENING — SECOND STEP

6°   *A black and red square beneath the ground*
Sociable, even-tempered. Feels need for material security for home and family. Enjoys competition. Very proud. Often senses the mystery of spiritual submission, but tends to give way to the outer feelings. Thorough, creative, with many interests.

7°   *A man speaks two languages fluently*
Sociable, versatile, talkative, exuberant, sometimes excitable. Tolerant, and capable of seeing both sides of an argument. Likes to act as go-between, but not always diplomatic. Enjoys hard work. Takes pride in doing two things at once.

8°   *A beribboned hat is tinted by the rising sun*
Unusual person. Sometimes appears frivolous with a jolly exterior, but very serious inwardly. Conscientious. Unconcerned with others' opinions. Selfless leader. Very optimistic despite inner conflicts. Aware instinctively of soul.

9°   *A fortune teller gazes into a crystal ball*
Tends to find submission to the inner life a strain, though there is a strong element of intuition. Physical needs may be neglected. Eager to learn, able to grasp complicated matters and make decisions. Good at understanding others.

10°   *Ancient symbols are being reinterpreted*
Unusually inward-looking for an Arien. Tends to prefer ideas to facts, but good at understanding root causes. Apt to neglect family and friends in favour of strangers. Puts great value on the inner life, and sometimes feels isolated.

ARIES

AWAKENING — THIRD STEP

11°   *A foreign ruler pays a state visit*
An idealist, setting high moral tone. Very proud, feels destined to lead. Tends to hurt others' feelings, but without malice. Outer personality somewhat at variance with inner feelings. Can be ruthless. Very much a traditional conformist.

12°   *A skein of geese fly through the clear, cold sky*
Very emotional, changeable character. Can change quickly from a state of languor to a whirl of activity. Values feelings above thoughts, but likes to present a practical image. Strong sensual desires and vivid imagination. Rarely bored.

13°   *A terrorist's bomb has been safely defused*
Uneasy character with great nervous energy. Seldom truly at peace. Creative through powerful imagination. Likes to present a carefree image. Has spiritual aspirations, but these tend to be governed by the brain, which causes unease.

14°   *A man, a woman, and a snake in sensual embrace*
The intellect is valued above emotions, which are seen as a sign of weakness. Very outward-looking and ambitious. Feels need to leave a permanent personal mark on the world. Liable to neglect spiritual values, and harbour a sense of grievance.

15°   *An old tribesman weaves a basket as the sun sets*
Independent, intense, physically oriented person. Has ability to put aggression to useful work. Generous in cases of suffering. Great practical ingenuity in using unpromising material, and learns from mistakes. Indulges sexual curiosity.

ARIES

WATCHING — FIRST STEP

16°   *Elves dance in the flickering firelight*
An unusual character with a powerful imagination. Not averse to
hard work. A frivolous and a sober side seem to pull in opposite
directions. Possesses a powerful but sometimes lazy intellect.
Creative, but can be over-impulsive.

17°   *Two elderly spinsters make polite conversation*
Sensitive character. Tends to suffer from emotional tension causing
inhibitions, particularly in early youth. Self sufficient, but needs
supportive family life. Sometimes appears intolerant. Becomes
more serene and poised in later life.

18°   *An empty hammock swings between two trees*
Competitive character, often physically brave. Can be aggressive
when necessary. Loves challenges, but takes back seat when these
are absent. Sociable, but finds social pleasantries irksome. With
broad sexual tastes, enjoys shocking people.

19°   *A magic carpet floats over a grimy industrial area*
Self confident, ambitious, can seem ruthless, but feelings can be
very light. Seldom afraid to have a go. Reasonably content
personally, but feels strongly for those less fortunately placed.
Opportunities sometimes wasted in pipe dreams.

20°   *A young girl feeds ducks beside a frozen pond*
Optimistic and happy, but rather quiet and apparently lonely. Never
withdrawn, but less outgoing than most Ariens. Emotional feelings
run deep. Compassionate, generous, patient and tactful. Tends to
lose reserve unexpectedly for a while.

ARIES

WATCHING — SECOND STEP

21°   *A champion boxer confidently climbs into the ring*
An assertive, self-confident character. Usually strong physically, mentally and emotionally. Daring, loves competition. When physique fails to match aspirations, strength becomes diverted to an inner drive. A reliable friend and a ruthless enemy.

22°   The gateway to a garden of delight
Reflective, almost wistful character. Would like to experience everything, good or bad, but is restrained by morality. Gives impression of innocence. Initial ambitions tend to fade out. Spiritual worth is understood and valued intuitively.

23°   *A young girl takes a neighbour's baby for a walk*
A contradictory character. Brave, conscientious and outwardly confident, has desire to succeed in competition, but emotions and bodily senses tend to shrink from real contact. Potential strength is in the inner plane. Tends to be opinionated.

24°   *Fresh air blows into a room, stirring the curtains*
Hopeful, visionary character with great faith in the future. Tends to project forthright image as leader and trend-setter to mask true nature, which is very private. Greatly aware of religious needs and the potential for spiritual expansion.

25°   *A parable has both a physical and a spiritual meaning*
A serious, literal-minded character. Great sense of destiny, and a good judge of others. Socially responsible, but likes to shock. Feels strong division between materiality and spirituality. Spiritual aims increase later in life.

ARIES

WATCHING — THIRD STEP

26°   *A wealthy benefactor, both proud and generous*
Confident, effervescent and outward looking. Possesses an affinity to wealth, but generous. Head and heart equally strong, and when they pull in opposite directions bad temper ensues. Entertains few self-doubts, and enjoys giving advice.

27°   *A marksman at first misses and then hits his target*
Independent, self-reliant character. Likes to present an image of calm assurance. Feels need to provide material security, but acutely aware of intangible values. Likes to speculate and learns well from experience, with ability to spot possible flaws.

28°   *A religious reformer shatters old idols*
A great reformer and innovator. Adaptable and full of ideas. Tends to speak too frankly at times. Very courageous, will confront formidable opponents, often using ridicule as a weapon. Often feels insecure, but seldom despairs.

29°   *In a dream, choirs of angels sing*
A self-assured optimist with a vivid imagination. Has a strong spirit of adventure, particularly inward exploration and all new experiences. Can be stubborn, and sometimes ignores unpleasant truths. Intuition increases with age.

30°   *Ducklings are learning to dabble on a pond*
Friendly, easy-going and sociable. Great capacity for enjoyment but not given to emotional display, sometimes appearing phlegmatic. More complicated than usually suspected, with very private feelings. Home-loving, responsible, sympathetic.

TAURUS

FEELING — FIRST STEP

31°   *A mountain stream rushes through a rocky glen*
A powerful, confident character. Emotional and moody, unusually sincere, with an enigmatic air of innocence. Serene on the surface whilst turbulent beneath. Strong pioneering instinct. Very persistent, with strong aims and ideals.

32°   *Sheet lightning flickers on the horizon*
A serenely uncomplicated character. Tolerant, with a strong sense of duty. Great capacity for hard work. A traditionalist. Intuitive in relating to others, preferring tact to force. A natural sense of wonder may obscure spiritual impulses.

33°   *Lush pasturelands rise into the foothills*
Calm, peaceful and responsible, socially oriented. Fond of family circle and very faithful. Values mutual support but needs to be alone when in introspective mood. Aware of faults and the need to remedy them. Cautious but receptive.

34°   *A pot of gold gleams at the rainbow's end*
Emotional character. An altruist, will support any cause seen as worthy. Great sense of personal worth, but little sense of family responsibility. Often torn between conscience and social requirements. Usually successful and resourceful.

35°   *A young widow returns home after the funeral*
A fatalist, with an odd air of angry wistfulness. Very aware of the suffering in the world. Humanitarian ideals powerful enough to overrule personal needs and obscure spiritual possibilities. Has a great admiration for the past. Plans well for the future.

TAURUS

FEELING— SECOND STEP

36°   *A bridge is being built over a ravine*
Explosive, quixotic temperament. An innovator who loves solving problems and faces challenges eagerly. Sometimes contemptuous of commonly accepted values. Has an intuitive sense of high purpose. Tends to be pragmatic regarding ethical problems.

37°   *The woman of Samaria draws water from the well*
A patient, serenely calm character. Emotions take precedence over thoughts. Confident in own decisions. Sensitive to others' feelings. Hates injustice. Can be over-emotional. Possesses powerful sex impulses. Often tends to be religious in an unconventional sense.

38°   *A sledge is drawn over dry mountain grass*
Individualistic pioneering character. Believes in free speech and frank expression. Can be impatient and tactless, but highly principled. Feels conflict between the need to conform, and rebellion against dogma. Rarely accepts defeat.

39°   *A decorated Christmas tree, surrounded by gifts*
Quiet character with powerful emotions. Usually kind and gentle. Can be impulsive, but decisions usually taken with care. Dislikes tedious routine. Tends to progress from youthful materiality to mature spiritual interests.

40°   *An attractive young nurse goes about her work*
Very sociable. Compassionate and a natural giver. Brave and cheerful in the face of adversity. Believes that principles should override personal considerations. Can be critical of others and this causes resentment. More tolerant later in life.

TAURUS

FEELING — THIRD STEP

41°   *A woman waters flowers in her garden*
An intense, sometimes over-emotional character. A powerful communicator, though not a great talker. Material security does not seem important. Unpractical, but may feel creative urges. Sensations seem important for happiness.

42°   *A young married couple plan for the future*
An outgoing person, sociable and very stable. Often ambitious, and usually achieves aims. Often thought materialistic, but realistic. Discriminating, with a strong sense of fair play. Disapproves of transitory pleasures. True to ideals.

43°   *A cheerful porter carries a stack of baskets*
Self-reliant and confident, with a zestful approach to life. Willing to work hard. Rather restless, but basically happy. Emotions run deep, but the thoughts take precedence. Clever at overcoming opposition. Sometimes possesses a fanatical sense of duty.

44°   *Children paddle and play as shellfish grope for food*
A strange and somewhat moody character. Emotional. Perceptive and penetrating when in a positive mood. Sometimes seems coarse or irreligious, but has sound understanding of spiritual values. Enjoys meeting people. Powerful sex drive.

45°   *A theatregoer in evening dress braves a storm*
More extraverted than most Taureans, with immense capacity for enjoyment. Believes introspection to be morbid and sees no need to self-explore deeply. Honest, hates hypocrisy. Values thoughts and sensations at the expense of emotions.

TAURUS

ENJOYMENT — FIRST STEP

46° *A wise old man tries to make his voice heard*
A quiet character, often highly intelligent. Enjoys complex problems. Thoughts tend to take precedence over emotions. Tends to see emotion as weakness, and neglects feelings. Friendly, kindly disposed to others. May feel isolated and often lonely.

47° *A battle rages between the forces of might and right*
A good all-rounder, intellectually, emotionally, and socially. A natural crusader and a good organizer. Attracted to group activities, but needs a quiet, private pursuit as well. May seem aggressive in youth, but becomes spiritually-oriented later.

48° *A woman is airing her linen in the sun*
A strangely restless person, seldom satisfied, always seeking improvement. Can be painfully honest with self, and critical of weakness in others. Quick to reject passing fads and artificial conventions. Good at analyzing problems.

49° *A new continent rises from the ocean*
Very solid, almost impregnable character, with a great sense of the need for security. Feels that struggle makes for healthy development. Thinking capacity overrules emotions, and can be unsympathetic through seeing emotion as weakness.

50° *Wispy clouds like streamers spread across the sky*
A strangely mystical character, often thought odd. An intuitive with very light feelings. May seem woolly-brained but very broad-minded. Kind and tolerant, though highly moral personally. Optimistic, hard-working, but not very practical.

TAURUS

ENJOYMENT — SECOND STEP

51°   *A mysterious finger underlines passages in a book*
A practical, down to earth character. Strongly principled, tends to be dogmatic. Able to see straight to the heart of a matter. A bold reformer who learns constructively from mistakes. Thinking takes precedence, and feelings may become repressed.

52°   *A homing pigeon flies low across rough sea*
Adventurous person with great energy. Eager for new experiences, often very physical. Takes pleasures very seriously. A free-thinker not bound by moral codes. The emotions may be neglected. Strong sex drive. Not very sympathetic.

53°   *A jeweler's shop, lavishly stocked.*
Self-sufficient character with an original turn of mind. A technological achiever, usually finding opportunities to use talents. Has great confidence, strong in adversity. Emotions are apt to suffer neglect. Prone to unfortunate love affairs.

54°   *A slightly built man drives a juggernaut truck.*
A rather diffident character. May appear distant, but friendly and easy-going at heart. Has great practical ability, but ideas usually seem more important than facts. Scrupulously loyal, but seldom accepts others on their own valuation.

55°   *A large and well-kept civic park*
A sociable character, strong-willed, with the basic urge to succeed. Usually has a keen brain, and takes an analytical approach to problems. Never shirks responsibilities, and likes to be relied upon. Has great moral strength. Dislikes sudden change.

TAURUS

ENJOYMENT — THIRD STEP

56°   *A Spaniard serenades his loved one at her balcony*
Intensely emotional character, drawing strength from the feelings. Alternates between emotional tension and deep peace. Possesses original and active imagination. Often ambitious. Adaptable, but can withdraw into a shell when desires are thwarted.

57°   *A proud tribal survivor sells tourist mementoes*
A very sincere and private person. Sometimes displays a false front as a defense mechanism. Versatile and creative, possessing ideals of wisdom and beauty, enjoying quiet, studious pursuits. A lover of old-time values. Not short of common sense.

58°   *A mature woman discovers a fresh romance*
Responsible, optimistic character. Like to feel in charge of own destiny. Seldom dismayed by hardship. A hard worker, mentally and physically. Cares deeply for the well-being of others. May be rebellious in youth, becoming realistic later.

59°   *Two cobblers are talking animatedly as they work*
A talkative lover of debate, with the natural ability to entertain. Thinking takes precedence, and the emotions are apt to be neglected. Feels an urge to explore and analyze. Often talented, but disputes over details may leave talents thwarted.

60°   *With spread tail, a peacock struts across the lawn*
A sincere, frank character, and a great reformer. Often thought iconoclastic, but in fact usually religious, and with an urge to retain ancient truths may seem to mock the traditions of others. Sometimes likes to shock, but judgment usually sound.

GEMINI

DESIRE — FIRST STEP

61°   *A glass-bottomed boat drifts over a coral reef*
An energetic person, plunging wholeheartedly into activity. Tends to extraversion in company, and introversion when alone. Feelings are kept private. Very aware of short-comings. May reject religion but values basic spirituality.

62°   *Toys are being purchased for a children's party*
A quietly self-assured character who takes pride in modesty. A natural benefactor. Emotional, sincere, sympathetic, practical. Will sacrifice comfort to a worthy cause. Tends to pre-judge others and lose temper easily. Tends to harbour cynical thoughts.

63°   *Aristocratic courtiers stroll through palace grounds*
A proud and optimistic person, outwardly contented but often uneasy inwardly. Thinking takes precedence over feelings. May appear unsympathetic, but in fact cares deeply for others. Sometimes over-reliant on moral rules and social customs.

64°   *Holly and mistletoe are brought indoors for Christmas*
Warm and unpretentious, but with a confusing duality of nature: a thinking side that needs progress, and an emotional side satisfied with the *status quo*. Fond of comforts. A good communicator ready to watch and learn.

65°   *A bold reformer preaches radical action*
An intense, poised, stable character. Thinking, feeling and sensation evenly balanced. Sincere, with a creative imagination, but often fails to see opposing viewpoints. Likes to cultivate relationships, and feels a need to enlighten society in general.

GEMINI

DESIRE — SECOND STEP

66°   *An oil platform is drilling through the night*
An active and energetic person, happy amidst bustle. A great competitor. The intuitive and thinking faculties are in balance, but emotions tend to be neglected. A perfectionist who expects others to toe the line. Usually successful but can be obsessive.

67°   *An old well, sheltered beneath tall tree*
A carefree character, poised and assured. Can be fierce when aroused. Receptive to the problems of others. Has a very keen brain, but both feeling and sensation are highly developed. Conscientious in a highly individual way, but may appear unprincipled.

68°   *Massed pickets assemble at a strike-bound pit*
A strangely fervent, sincere character. Strong willed and full of ideals, with an immense capacity for hard work. Does not greatly care for material gain. Possesses a keen brain, but seldom listens to opposing arguments. Needs to participate in action.

69°   *An archer draws his bow, prepared to kill*
Single minded, tenacious, determined and very independent, a character who sees life as a struggle for advancement. Can be very aggressive, but totally loyal. Traditions mean little. Powerful emotions are restrained by an astute brain.

70°   *A light plane pulls out of a steep dive*
Purposeful, daring, independent character. One of the most active Geminians. Works hard to overcome difficulties. Can be reckless. Loves new experiences and opportunities. Self-motivating, expecting others to be equally zealous.

GEMINI

DESIRE — THIRD STEP

71°   *Newly settled virgin lands await cultivation*
A fiercely protective character who takes responsibilities seriously. Thinking is the most active function, with strong undercurrents of emotion. Possesses powerful opinions and a dislike of secrets. A pioneering spirit, but of the armchair type.

72°   *A slave girl confronts her mistress boldly*
An oddly innocent character, alternating between astuteness and naivety. Ambitious and fatalistic. Emotion plays little part in life, nevertheless a well balanced person psychologically. Possesses an unsuspectedly calculating turn of mind: a good judge.

73°   *A virtuoso pianist begins his concert*
An individualistic character, very ambitious with great staying power. Motivated by the emotions, regulated by the mind. Aims to please others and often holds great influence over them. Sometimes moody, and often seems pitted against the world.

74°   *Thought transference occurring between two people*
A quietly ambitious person who values close-knit relationships. Lover of mysteries, interested in ancestry and the past. Thoughts take precedence over emotions which may be neglected. ssometimes impractical but usually resourceful.

75°   *In a schoolroom, two children study together*
A broad-minded liberal with a clearly defined set of values. Patient, but ready to seize opportunities as they arise. Strong emotional undercurrent, often seeing profound meanings in life. Forthright, but can tactfully withhold opinions.

GEMINI

STRIVING — FIRST STEP

76°   *A woman agitator harangues a crowd*
A strangely restless character. Tense inwardly even when outwardly peaceful. Intellectually outgoing, yet with powerful introverted intuitive faculty. Always aware of hidden depths to life. Can become irritable, but seldom malicious.

77°   *A wise old man and a youth walk side by side*
Temperamental character, sometimes reserved, sometimes unrestrained. Sincere and basically very private. Emotions tend to flow inwards, but able to think clearly. Firm personal values always seeking the best available. Often artistically talented.

78°   *Inscrutable easterners visit the west*
Independent, self-contained, quick witted. With thoughts turning outwards, tends to equate deep emotion with sincerity, and enjoys stirring strong feelings. Highly principled. Sometimes over-protective. Often generous to a fault. A lover of luxury.

79°   *An ancient ornate book in a museum*
A restless character, though outwardly stable. Usually silent in company. A deep thinker, able to take familiar ideas and give them a new creative slant. Like to keep full extent of knowledge private. Believes in equality, and respects all cultures.

80°   *A buffet luncheon with a lavish variety of food*
Versatile, practical, sensible, often physically talented. Thorough and not averse to hard work. Takes pride in producing the best. Often artistic. Seldom courts popularity, but still happy to bathe in acclaim. Meets challenges boldly and optimistically.

GEMINI

STRIVING — SECOND STEP

81°   *Demonstrators chant rhythmically in a city street*
A zealous, competitive character. Possesses strong emotions which
are directed outwards, but believes that logical thought is in charge.
A good organizer, and a believer in fair shares for all. Keenly
imaginative and practical.

82°   *Merry country dancing follows the harvest*
Sociable, versatile, responsible, an extravert at work and an
introvert at home. Thoughts directed towards material
achievements, feelings confined to leisure and home. Often feels
innately superior to others. Often highly talented. Remains faithful
within the family.

83°   *Fledglings peer out from their nest*
A confident person, mentally agile, manually dexterous, brave and
physically orientated. Ever seeking new opportunities, and able to
see into the heart of matters. Eager to investigate unknown
potential and experiment. Not averse to a little deception.

84°   *Children are skating on a frozen pond*
A happy, self-contained character. Rarely ambitious, an admirer of
simplicity. Might be thought naive and unfeeling, but the emotions
are kept well cloaked. Generous in material terms. Tends to see the
good in people and situations and ignore obvious faults.

85°   *A gardener lovingly prunes his flowering shrubs*
A positive thinker who tends to suppress the emotions. May seem
uncaring and apt to retreat from close relationships. Tends to hide
beliefs behind formulas, but able to assess the odds keenly enough.
Usually successful, but avoids luxury.

GEMINI

STRIVING — THIRD STEP

86°   *The frosty tracery of winter trees*
An optimist with a constructive imagination. Able to see beauty and goodness in unpromising situations. Thinking is the chief function, but the emotions are also powerful. Adaptable and determined. Sympathetic to others' problems.

87°   *A gipsy child watches distant school children at play*
An eager, pioneering character with a sense of unfulfilled longing, never completely satisfied. Self confidence grows with the years. Seldom able to relax fully, often feeling frustrated. A powerful imagination reinforces ambitions.

88°   *Released by the courts, a man faces the world*
A very stable character physically and mentally. Likes to express thoughts openly whilst seeming emotionally uninvolved, but in fact the emotions run deep. Times of crisis bring out the best, but tends to neglect practicalities such as financial obligations.

89°   *Song birds herald the arrival of spring*
An eager, vivacious character. Gregarious, but if socializing too freely feels guilty of over-indulgence. Quick thinking, versatile and reliant with multiple interests. usually seems to be in a hurry. Tends to value spoken rather than written words.

90°   *A beauty contest is being held on the beach*
A somewhat contradictory character. Has a quick brain with outgoing thoughts but private and introverted feelings. Seldom seems well-adjusted socially. Possesses a great capacity for the spiritual dimension. Self-critical. Able to see both sides of an argument.

CANCER

DARING — FIRST STEP

91°   *A sailor hoists a new flag*
Self-confident, ambitious character dedicated to success. Takes a bold, eager approach to life. Outwardly restless, inwardly patient. Unusually sensitive to spiritual ideas. Sympathetic and receptive, but realistic. Very conscientious. Generous, sensitive to the needs of others.

92°   *Hang-gliding, a man watches people far below*
A steady, stolid character. Socially confident, enjoys an audience more than most Cancerians. Sets thoughts above emotions and has great powers of reasoning. Looks at life objectively. Very conscientious, generous, and sensitive to the needs of others.

93°   *An arctic explorer drives his dog team*
A difficult person to understand. Bold and impetuous, yet with a quality of innocence. Enjoys frequent changes of lifestyle. Not very interested in personal gratification. Sensitive to atmosphere and likes to hear about the ideas of others. Usually modest in all things.

94°   *A revolutionary committee condemns opponents*
A home-loving person, faithful to the intimate circle but unconcerned with outsiders. Often highly intelligent and witty in argument. Seeks solace in intimacy. Seldom suffers from self-doubt. Unswerving once convinced, and sometimes becomes fanatical.

95°   *A car driver races a train to the crossing*
A conscientious intuitive whose relationships are sometimes chaotic. Possesses burning zeal and powerful principles which sometimes lead to neglect of personal relationships. Often critical of judgment, sometimes hurtful and forceful.

CANCER

DARING — SECOND STEP

96°   *A colony of birds are building their nests*
A steadfast, reliable, sweet-tempered character with a penetrating mind. Seldom lazy, but may dissipate energy in dreams when ambitions are thwarted. Strives to acquire material security. Needs the support of a partner to make best efforts in life.

97°   *Two elves are dancing in a moonlit woodland glade*
A versatile character, intuitive and imaginative. Responsible, but can seem flippant in serious situations. Broad-minded, but can be over-critical of others. Not very modest and may seem conceited. Kind at heart, but can seem callous at times.

98°   *A homely woman reads a glossy fashion magazine*
A warm, sympathetic, conscientious character, acutely aware of injustices. Honest with intimate circle, but may put on a show for outsiders. Capable of hard sustained efforts. Usually content, but subject to vague fears and doubts.

99°   *A naked child tries to catch a goldfish*
A strangely innocent character, without pretence, adopting an eager approach to life. Scrupulously careful in making decisions, likes to take responsibility. Oriented mainly towards emotional feeling, and tends to neglect practical considerations.

100°   *A magnificent diamond is being cut to shape*
A practical, versatile character. Calm, almost phlegmatic, but never dull. Ethical, civilized, rarely makes mistakes. Kind, but can be hard when necessary. Exudes self-assurance which less fortunate people sometimes find annoying.

CANCER

DARING — THIRD STEP

101°   *An impressionist makes fun of well-known people*
A contradictory character, outwardly frivolous, inwardly serious. A certain shyness is well hidden behind social poise and affected indifference. Able to see through the pretences of others. Needs to feel well thought-of. Always prefers making own decisions.

102°   *A baby lies chuckling on a bright yellow blanket*
A vivacious character with a healthy physical awareness. Thinking and feeling functions are well in balance. Seems to possess insight into hidden truths, but eager to experience and learn. Often displays a great love for living creatures. Enjoys material comforts.

103°   *A hand is held out to receive*
A reserved character, thoughtful and careful. Usually seems relaxed, but is often subject to nagging worries. Firm moral convictions lead to a dislike for indulgence. Hard working, reliable and punctilious, equates risk-taking with instability.

104°   *A lonely old man faces the storm*
A well-adjusted character, sociable, self-reliant, inventive and usually talented. Good head for facts and figures. Feelings run strong but are rarely expressed openly. Undemons-trative. Tends to take family loyalty for granted.

105°   *Sated revelers rest after a banquet*
Generous, warm-hearted, responsible, down to earth. Reliably calm in a crisis, a well-balanced personality with deep emotions, but spiritual values may be underrated. Enjoys a life of luxury, but is able to make the best of circumstances.

CANCER

SINCERITY — FIRST STEP

106°   *A parchment scroll marked with a square*
An inflexible character. A precisionist who believes that rules must be observed. Robust and active, very down to earth. The intellect has priority over the emotions. Possesses a strong sense of duty but seems over-concerned with details.

107°   *A ship's pilot takes over the helm*
The feelings are directed inward, and the inner feelings are close to the surface. May be thought cold as emotions rarely find outward expression. Is able to confront self with honesty. Remains faithful to principles, but believes practical experience to be the best guide.

108°   *A clucking hen is leading her chicks*
An enigmatic character, emotional, defensive, sympathetic and generous. Often takes the problems of others to heart. Values simple joys, but is always constructively practical. May be short-tempered. Needs a close and devoted circle of friends.

109°   *An upper-class girl marries a working-class boy*
A born leveler. Emotion is the chief function, usually confident and friendly. Feels guilty if born to wealth, and a sense of injustice if born to poverty. May scorn commonly-accepted values. A true romantic with an inbuilt feeling of moral superiority.

110°   *A party of holiday makers take a ride in a gondola*
A romantic traditionalist. Sociable, kind-hearted with practical sympathy. Rarely strict on morality, but likes to adhere to the rules. Adventurously versatile. Capable of unselfish love, but dislikes sentiment. May seem unrealistic to outsiders.

CANCER

SINCERITY — SECOND STEP

111°   *A prima donna sings to a glittering audience*
A confident, physically assured extravert. Hardworking with boundless energy, fearless in the face of provocation, always seeking new experiences. Tends to ignore intellectual values, relying on emotions. Loves attention and physical activity.

112°   *A child watches a sailing boat entering the harbour*
A contradictory character, torn between progress and restraint, outgoing urges checked by an inner resistance. Favours quiet intellectual pursuits, often with an artistic slant. Usually self-sufficient, and capable of achieving perfection in the chosen field.

113°   *In a learned society a debate is taking place*
A self-confident, intellectual character. Diplomatic, but never slow to reap any personal benefits. Possesses a great sense of pride and self-worth. Loves innocent, delicate and beautiful things. Sometimes seems oddly naive. Weighs facts carefully before speaking.

114°   *A castaway sits on a desert island, staring out to sea*
An uneasy character, oddly fragmented, with thoughts, emotions and sensations all pulling in different directions. Stability and confidence grow with the years. At best in sympathetic company. Often worries unnecessarily. Often strongly attracted to religion.

115°   *Superman the hero makes his identity known*
A physical and intellectual adventurer. A natural leader, with an oddly innocent demeanour. Happily sociable, with a knack of spreading feelings of confidence. Gladly takes on responsibilities, gaining insight and gravity with the years.

CANCER

SINCERITY — THIRD STEP

116°   *Guests are browsing in the library of a stately home*
Effervescent character, mentally quick and penetrating. Able to change point of view easily but with sincerity. Feels sympathy for good and bad alike. At times seems filled with strange ideas, but has a realistic understanding of own personal capabilities.

117°   *A thunder storm rages through a rocky valley*
A determined achiever, capable of taking quite alarming chances. Seldom ready to admit defeat, but apt to lose interest quickly and change course. Full of ambitious ideas. Tends to keep feelings hidden. Strong sense of objective value. Inwardly a tranquil type.

118°   *A black girl takes her white boy friend home*
A natural iconoclast who hates traditional fixed ideas. Often thought outrageous, but very sincere, with a powerful dislike of hypocrisy. A wise judge in material matters, but tends to be irresponsible in matters of the heart.

119°   *Royal twins described in a fairy tale*
An enigmatic character, unorthodox, sometimes vague, sometimes matter-of-fact. Possesses a powerfully creative imagination. Loves exploring new ideas. Needs an intimate circle of friends and is somewhat cold with outsiders. Needs to feel fulfilled.

120°   *An aristocratic lady delivers an after-dinner speech*
A confident traditionalist with an inbuilt sense of benevolent superiority. Entertains few self doubts, and actions generally above reproach. Loves to lead and set the pace. Enjoys a modicum of elaborate ceremonial. Usually pious.

LEO

CONVICTION — FIRST STEP

121° *A furious man, his blood pressure high*
Very active character with a great sense of urgency. Competitive with a need to achieve and lead. Highly principled but not inflexible. Gregarious. Pure hearted. Tends to equate laziness with sinfulness. Often short tempered, but patience grows with years.

122° S*chool closed, the children amuse themselves*
A free thinker with the potential for either greatness or chaos. Can be fanatical. Clever and versatile but unpredictable, often changing course dramatically. May seem preoccupied with the need for social change. Often charitable. Serene in later life.

123° *A middle-aged woman admires her new hair style*
An introspective but happily sociable person. Optimistic and confident, with great powers of reasoning. Very energetic. Believes in teamwork but often stands out from the crowd. Ready to learn by experience and admit mistakes.

124° *An elderly gentleman admires his club's trophies.*
A solid traditionalist with impeccable taste. Confident, witty and intellectual. Seldom changes mind, but always ready to listen to opposing views. Enjoys energetic pursuits. A loving family person, kind to those in need. Tends to over-value wealth.

125° *Rock pillars stand like statues overlooking a valley*
A thoughtful person with powerful sensations. Realistic, usually thought reliable. Can be over-indulgent but sometimes lacking in tact and compassion. Calm and confident, almost phlegmatic. Family circle is important and a source of pride.

LEO

CONVICTION — SECOND STEP

126° *A fashion model admires a gorgeous Victorian dress*
An efficient idealist. Honest, sincere, and physically brave, can be aggressive. A good organizer and leader with few self -doubts. Gives and demands loyalty. Feels the need to achieve power, even at the expense of disrupting others. Sometimes nostalgic.

127° *The stars are brilliant in the desert sky*
A character of great intellectual heights and emotional depths. Capable of introspection, a vivid imagination put to constructive use. Will give generously, but often fails to notice the need. Patient, with a vague sense of mysticism.

128° *An agitator harangues the crowd with passion*
A somewhat troubled character, always acting for the best but running into opposition. Can be loyal to friends and ruthless with enemies. Always feels need to change things for the better. A good improviser. Can be moody. Despises materialistic attitudes.

129° *Glass blowers create strange glowing shapes*
An intensely emotional but down-to-earth character. Dependable, with an inbuilt desire to do good in the world. Can be resentful when others fail to respond. A good provider with a close family circle. Enjoys comforts, and can seem self-satisfied.

130° *Dew sparkles beneath the rising sun*
A light-hearted, spontaneous character. Friendly and never superior, but sets high standards of conduct. Intuitive, with ability to think problems through. Possesses great understanding and compassion for those in need. Gregarious. Determined.

LEO

CONVICTION — THIRD STEP

131°   *Children are playing beneath a shady tree*
A proud and somewhat guarded character, deeply and privately emotional. Warm-hearted beneath the restraint. Conceals sentiment beneath a layer of logic. Appears cultured but tends to mock refinement. Obstinate, impulsive, often indulgent.

132°   *A garden party lit by Chinese lanterns*
An inflexible character, not at all modest, and with a great sense of self-worth. Very sociable, brimming with self-confidence. Usually respected and admired. Tends not to learn from experience. Organized leisure and hard work given equal importance.

133°   *A retired skipper watches the sea through his window*
A proud character, never shy, but strangely retiring for a Leo. Inventive, self-reliant, a skilful delegator. Loves authority and making decisions. Appears hesitant before plunging in whole-heartedly. Failures avoided by prudent withdrawal.

134°   *An unborn child is kicking in the womb*
Vivacious character, friendly and fun-loving. Often athletic, with a great need to communicate. Loves luxury and may waste resources on entertainment. Rarely interested in cultural pursuits, though more thoughtful in later life. Not given to speculation.

135°   *An ethnic carnival throngs the city streets*
A light-hearted, naturally innocent character. May seem irresponsible, but thoroughly honest. Can sometimes be self-indulgent or promiscuous. Impatient with criticism. Happy and sociable. In old age passions give way to quiet serenity.

LEO

EXPLANATION — FIRST STEP

136° *The countryside smells sweetly after a rainstorm*
A proud, self-assured person who can appear self-satisfied. Intelligent. Enjoys good things but retains a sense of moderation. Well able to recover from difficulties and start afresh. Can be very patient. Feels drawn towards spiritual knowledge.

137° *A church congregation hold a coffee morning*
A hard-working character, reliant and optimistic. Sociable, enjoys participating. Feels a need to preserve the *status quo* and tends to equate right with might. Entertains few self-doubts. Believes in predestination. Can seem intolerant at times, but hates injustice.

138° *A scientist conducts a practical experiment*
A dignified, confident character. Proud of achievements. Never falsely modest but dislikes the glare of publicity. One of the quietest of Leos. Able to see to the heart of a problem, and loves to uncover hidden secrets. Conscientious, hates delegation.

139° *Merrymakers sing together aboard a pleasure boat*
A sociable, creative character who sees life as a joyful struggle. Works and plays hard and dislikes retiring types. Can seem clannish, and broodingly discontent when the standard of living drops below par. Intelligent, but not analytical by nature.

140° *Motionless Druids watch the rising of the sun*
A serenely optimistic character, confident of own personal judgment. Broad-minded, but has a great sense of propriety. Mystically orientated, but not necessarily religious. A proud Leo who entertains few self-doubts.

LEO

EXPLANATION — SECOND STEP

141°   *Farm animals become intoxicated on windfall apples*
A somewhat inconsistent character who tends to dip into everything but ends up satisfied with nothing. Good at seeing to the core of a problem, but somewhat woolly emotions tend to over-cloud intellectual judgment. May pursue illogical courses.

142°   *A homing pigeon returns at dawn*
A broad-minded free-thinker. Thinking is the chief faculty and emotions are largely ignored. Possesses great energy. A natural explorer who feels the need for a comfortable base. A feeling of moral superiority tends to belittle others.

143°   *An acrobatic rider performs in the circus*
A well-controlled character, with a capacity for both robust enjoyment and quiet pursuits. Physically brave and hard-working, with the sensitive vision of a poet. Always tries to operate on a grand scale, and may sometimes fall spectacularly, though seldom defeated.

144°   *An Indian fakir, unwashed and ragged*
An oddly intense character to whom ideas are more important than emotions or physical sensations. Usually completely virtuous, ignoring sensual desires. Cares deeply about what others may think, which may lead to recklessness or fanaticism.

145°   *A lone Arab crosses the desert on his camel*
A natural analyst and logician who believes that the intellect should govern the emotions. Can appear to lack warmth, but traditional home standards are important. Versatile, brave, seldom shirks duty and will tolerate hardship uncomplainingly.

LEO

EXPLANATION — THIRD STEP

146°   As t*he storm passes a rainbow appears*
A self-confident optimist, emotional, charming and sympathetic. Always ready to help those in need. Takes pride in caring, but cares little for principles. Always values strength of feeling and distrusts intellectuals. Resourceful when necessary.

147°   *The stars slowly fade as dawn breaks*
A practical character. Likes to be though intellectual, and loves giving advice. Appreciates a touch of ceremony and grandeur. Can seem flamboyant, often artistic. Can be generous, but does not care to become deeply involved in others' problems.

148°   *A large flock of birds sing together on a tree*
A well-adjusted person, lively, confident, sociable and talkative. Loves travelling, visiting, and "keeping in touch". Capable of hard work behind the scenes. Often though frivolous, but possesses a great deal of pride, and likes to keep good deeds private.

149°   *A fairytale princess waits for her prince*
A contradictory character, confident in society but with nagging doubts inside. Normally happy and sociable, enjoying a touch of luxury. Can be morose when alone. Often haunted by fear of failure. Has an active brain. Usually admired by others.

150°   *An important and confidential letter is left unsealed*
An open, trusting character. Flamboyant, easy-going, kind-hearted, sincere and honest. Sometimes carries frankness to the point of naivety. May hurt people's feelings by trying to right imagined wrongs. Strong emotions overrule logic.

VIRGO

INVENTION — FIRST STEP

151° *A lifelike but flattering portrait*
A gregarious type, usually friendly, but dislikes solitary people who are thought morbid. For this reason is sometimes accused of superficiality. Quite philosophical, but over-conscious of the public image. Likes to think of mankind as one family.

152° *A solitary cross stands high on a rugged hill*
A scrupulously conscientious character. Reliable and hard-working. Very deep emotions, but tends to keep private feelings well hidden. Enjoys being the benefactor, and tends to become over-involved in the misfortunes of others.

153° *A pioneering family confidently build their first home*
A traditionalist who believes in responsibility and correct behaviour. Intuitive, able to foresee snags. Trusts own judgment, but professes faith in divine protection. Suffers hardship stoically, and always willing to learn from experience.

154° *Children of different races play happily together*
A great communicator, sociable and talkative. Relationships seem all-important. First class organizer, helpful and well-meaning, full of bright ideas. Capable of rising above personal shortcomings by recruiting others. Acutely aware of injustices.

155° *An Irishman thinks he sees a leprechaun under a tree*
A practical, efficient character. Logic takes precedence over emotions. Versatile, and able to put new ideas to work, but never too venturesome. Seldom introspective. Possesses a constructive imagination, and confidence in own ability to succeed.

VIRGO

INVENTION — SECOND STEP

156°   *Children on a blaring fairground ride*
An adventurous character who plunges boldly into life. Dislikes any personal weakness, but rather likes the weaknesses of others. Sincerely friendly. Enjoys good food and physical comforts. Tends not to learn from mistakes.

157°   *A sultan's wives gossip lazily in the harem*
An unpredictable character with artistic sensitivity. Romantically light-hearted. Emotions take precedence over intellect. Often erratic and irresponsible, but remains convinced of own personal dependability. Generous with moral but not material support.

158°   *A child wears a new school uniform*
An incorrigible rebel, forever trying out alternative ways. Often highly intelligent, but consistently ignores advice, good or bad, preferring to learn by practical experience. Strong willed and irresponsible in youth, becoming more stable and responsible later.

159°   *A newly-painted example of abstract art*
A staunch individualist who scorns the popular view. Often very clever, a logical and precise analyst who takes nothing for granted. Works and plays hard. Dislikes delegating responsibility. tends to ignore opposition, and faces problems courageously.

160°   *A man and his double walk side by side*
A shrewd. self-controlled character. A keen brain ready to grasp opportunities as they arise and usually successful in enterprises. Projects an air of serenity when others are panicking. Possesses great stamina.

VIRGO

INVENTION — THIRD STEP

161°   *A schoolboy helps his father build a garden shed*
Completely natural, open character, totally normal in tastes and
habits. Eminently practical. Very intuitive and quick to evaluate
opportunities. Seldom compromises strong principles. Loyal and
helpful, energetic when seeing a positive course to pursue.

162°   *An Indian groom gently lifts his bride's veil*
A venturesome character, full of self confidence. A keenly
analytical mind with a fund of unusual ideas. Loves mysteries. Has
few self-doubts, and is willing to be judged on own personal
merits. Proud of achievements, strong on matters of social
injustice.

163°   *Calmly, a statesman wins over an emotional crowd*
A calm even-natured character. A keen analytical brain keeps active
emotions under control. Often thought cold or unresponsive.
Possesses great faith in personal ability. May seem lazy, but works
hard when the cause is worthy.

164°   *An ancient family tree on a parchment scroll*
Very self-confident character with a great sense of tradition and
self-worth. Rarely suffers from doubts of any kind. Very sensitive
and proud, with deep feelings. Loyal and honest, capable of
maintaining high standards. Possesses a great sense of destiny.

165°   *A lace handkerchief, fine perfume, and a mirror*
A strangely divided character, with a mind that admires toughness,
a heart that admires delicacy. Feelings of insecurity are cloaked
with hard work. Likes to relax in luxury when possible, dropping
the hard veneer in intimate surroundings.

VIRGO

EXPERIMENTATION — FIRST STEP

166° *Students visit a retired college professor*
A peaceful character with powerful emotions and a keen brain. Quick to react, resourceful and adaptable. Self-assertive, and can seem uncaring. Possesses great faith in own judgment. Deep feelings tend to be equated with truth. Unflappable in crisis.

167° *A volcano suddenly erupts*
Volatile character, prone to sudden changes of attitude. Respects traditions, but tends to scoff at others' beliefs. Artistic. An eager participator. Usually optimistic but can suffer from nagging doubts. Hot-headed in youth but tranquility grows over the years.

168° *A spiritualist medium is holding a seance*
A proud and independent individualist. Powerfully enquiring mind tends to overlook emotional feelings. Can be critical both of self and others. Religiously unconventional. May well suffer from psychological trouble in middle years.

169° *An Olympic swimming event is under way*
A quiet character with a powerfully active brain and deep emotions. Often markedly introverted. Can seem absent-minded but often highly talented and quick to assimilate new ideas. Quietly competitive. Needs to feel approval, and tends to brood.

170° *An adventurer starts across the desert in an old car*
An eager, bustling character. Quick to rise to challenges, but emotionally undemonstrative. Keeps calm in emergencies. Faces hardship cheerfully, sacrificing short-term for long-term benefits. Able to discriminate wisely, and possesses an enduring faith.

VIRGO

EXPERIMENTATION — SECOND STEP

171°   *A girls' hockey match has begun*
Intuitive type with powerful emotions and sensual desires, tempered by a puritanical streak. Keen on fitness, moral, physical and spiritual. Tendency to brood and feel guilty over any self-indulgence. Tends to despise those who let their standards slip.

172°   *The crown jewels on display in the Tower of London*
A well-adjusted, poised, sociable, hard-working, conscien-tious character. Frequently over-indulges but seldom feels guilty about it. Sometimes thought conceited. Able to accept new ideas whilst adhering to old standards. Can be contemplative.

173°   *A Roman gladiator strides into the arena*
Confident character with a powerful will. Very active and physically brave. Can be argumentative and bad-tempered. A trusted leader able to master complex problems. Not a modest person, but always truthful. A perfectionist.

174°   *A book of nursery rhymes*
A very happy character of almost childlike simplicity. Friendly, fun-loving, prefers enjoyment to responsibilities. Uninhibited by social conventions. Imaginative and often creative. Always honest and not greatly ambitious, but has an active curious mind.

175°   *Above an embassy building, the flag flies at half-mast*
A brave but oddly hesitant character. Tends to draw back, the better to advance and tackle problems. Has strong mental powers, somewhat puritanical. Values traditions and possessions. Dislikes over-indulgence and keeps personal impulses well under control.

VIRGO

EXPERIMENTATION — THIRD STEP

176°   *A schoolboy plays a new computer game*
A happy, optimistic character. Possesses a keen mind, always probing and analyzing. Able to see beauty in dull, everyday things. Always young at heart. Capable of working hard, but may overlook the main issues. Patient and seldom critical.

177°   *A bishop entertains a lady to tea*
A strangely wistful character. Has considerable mental powers and creative imagination, but lacks confidence. Loyal and sympathetic, takes pride in status, but often feels under-valued. Able to view shortcomings philosophically.

178°   *A bald headed man chairs a national meeting*
An enigmatic somewhat tortured character with inward-turned conflicts. Has an analytical mind with firmness of purpose but seldom projects ideas outwards. Capable of hard sustained work. Becomes more tranquil and less introverted in later life.

179°   *An archeologist uncovers some ancient documents*
An eager, ambitious character. Very inventive with perceptive judgment. Persistent, a theorist fond of reappraising old values. Impatient with own weaknesses and keeps them hidden. Cares about people, but tends to neglect family and close friends.

180°   *Dull routine is broken by an emergency call*
A volatile, unpredictable character with a keen brain and powerful emotions. Tends to explode unexpectedly into action. Basically moral and often very religious. Sometimes self-indulgent. Tends to overlook own faults whilst criticizing others.

LIBRA

RUMINATION — FIRST STEP

181°   *A newly emerged butterfly opens its wings in the sun*
An innovator with an original turn of mind. Not very self-assured, and can seem oddly vulnerable. Confident when things are going well. Tends to present weaknesses as though they were virtues. Honest with self, less so with others. Loves variety.

182°   *An orchestra plays an epic symphony*
A proud but friendly character. Often strongly ambitious, loves to take the initiative and lead the way. Possesses deep emotions and a great sense of personal worth and destiny. A keen observer of people. Diplomatic, even when rejecting others' point of view.

183°   *Daybreak reveals a different world*
An enquiring, adventurous character. A versatile innovator with a vivid imagination. Hates humdrum routine. Emotional, and seems unpredictable. A natural peace-maker who seldom quarrels. Suffers conflict between adventurous impulses and the need for security.

184°   *A band of pilgrims sit silently around their camp fire*
A sincere, uncompromising character. High minded with deep emotions, convinced of rightness of purpose. Free of self-doubt. Likes to appear easy-going, but can be ruthless in following principles. Individualistic, but not a loner.

185°   *A class of mature students listen to their tutor*
A zealous character, always seeking new challenges. Often physically daring. An impatient risk-taker with strong ambitions. Emotions tend to be suppressed. Community minded, family life may be chaotic. A crusader who hates complacency.

LIBRA

RUMINATION — SECOND STEP

186°   *In a dream, hopes and wishes are fulfilled*
An anxious, yearning character, never completely satisfied. Feels a need to be accepted. Usually very practical and hard-working, with a constructive imagination. May become workaholic. Always looking for new opportunities.

187°   *A gamekeeper feeds the birds later to be shot*
A well-guarded, private character with great powers of concentration. Can seem ruthless, but likes to be unsentimental and seldom feels guilt. Capable of caring without strong attachments. Diplomatic, able to argue both sides of a case convincingly.

188°   *A welcoming fire glows in an empty, isolated house*
An undemonstrative character with great depths of emotion. Honest, but capable of ignoring unpalatable truths. Diplomatic, adaptable, conscientious, hard-working. Needs to feel that the good things of life are available, but seldom makes full use of them.

189°   *Three paintings hang in an art gallery*
A serene, unpretentious character, sociable, friendly, but partly reserved. Possesses great personal dignity and radiates a sense of gentle pride. An intellectual with well-controlled feelings. a giver rather than a taker, with little need for luxury.

190°   *A canoe leaves the rapids and enters calm water*
A calmly optimistic character. Ambitious in an undemon-strative way. Likes to be thought of as a thinker, but deep emotions are always to the fore. Capable of wild bouts of energy followed by tranquility. Reliable, seldom delegates responsibilities.

LIBRA

RUMINATION — THIRD STEP

191°   *An elderly teacher faces a class of young pupils*
A self-assured person with few self-doubts. Thinking is foremost, but intuition is often used. Tends to overvalue material worth. Values traditions highly and always sides with authority. Kind-hearted and tolerant of weakness, but may indulge in mockery.

192°   *Miners emerge from a pit shaft into daylight*
A confident, enquiring character always eager to learn. The thinking mind overrules the feelings which may be neglected. Loves to delve into mysteries and seldom takes facts at their face value. Very proud. Admires frankness and hates subterfuge.

193°   *At play-school, toddlers are blowing bubbles*
A calm, well-controlled type. Friendly, with an innocent sense of wonder. Physical sensations tend to take priority over reasoned ideas. Thoughts are kept private, and the emotional feelings tend to be overlooked. Sociable, open and indulgent.

194°   *In the tropics, a wealthy planter relaxes in his garden*
A proud, confident, self-sufficient type. Intuitive, likes to make opinions known but keeps emotions private. Very sensuous and sometimes permissive. Fond of luxury, feeling need for material security. Often clashes with higher authorities.

195°   *Precision-tooled wheels are stacked in a factory store*
An epicurean character with a keen brain, often seemingly over-concerned with the physical sensations. Indulgent, but takes careful stock beforehand. A good provider, sometimes seems obsessed with material possessions. Energetic and helpful.

LIBRA

DISCOVERY — FIRST STEP

196°   *A gang of workers cheerfully repair storm damage*
An eminently practical precisionist. Thinking is given priority and the feelings are often overlooked. Likes to be thought light-hearted, but dislikes frivolity, laziness and inefficiency. Often workaholic, using creative powers for financial gain.

197°   *A retired captain watches as his old ship sails away*
An enigmatic character. Usually seems deeply thoughtful, but main psychological functions are emotion and intuition. Quiet and unassuming, would secretly love to be free from moral restraints. Will often pursue some cause only to lose interest after a while.

198°   *Two prisoners are brought to trial*
A very emotional, unpredictable character. Very frank, quick to challenge authority. Seems to like shocking people, and yet worries greatly about what they might think. Seems poised between aggression and friendliness. Can be very generous.

199°   *A highwayman waits to ambush a stagecoach*
A fervently ambitious character, energetic, with a keen brain. Often physically daring. Can be ruthless in seeking gain. Possesses creative imagination which is put to useful purpose. Tends to overvalue differential between abilities and classes.

200°   *At peace, a scholarly rabbi consults his library*
A happy, peaceful character. A deep thinker whose feelings tend to be turned inwards. Responsible, genuinely charit-able. Feels quietly superior, but seldom looks for acclaim. Self-contained, able to withdraw within and be content.

LIBRA

DISCOVERY — SECOND STEP

201°   *On the promenade, holidaymakers enjoy sea breezes*
An ambitious, highly competitive character. Very keen intellect. Brave, purposeful, very confident, loves to be in the thick of action. Likes to be thought unyielding, seldom relaxed physically. The emotions are kept firmly under control. An efficient organizer.

202°   *A child, a mossy fountain, and a drinking bird*
A creative person with powerful emotions and strong intellect, with great physical awareness. Enjoys sensual pleasures with an innocent air and likes to be thought permissive, but never undignified in behaviour. Seldom takes self too seriously.

203°   *A cock crows at dawn*
A highly intuitive, sincere character. Valiant and true to personal values, ignores risks to do the right thing. Hates injustice, taking responsibilities very seriously. Accepts hardship without complaint. Likes to be respected as a leader.

204°   *A beautiful butterfly with a deformed wing*
A rather sad, wistful character. Emotional, but likes to be thought realistic and down to earth. Can seem over-dependent, and tends to feel isolated even in company. Aware of own short-comings Tends to waste opportunities and feel resentment.

205°   *School children shuffle through fallen autumn leaves*
An eager, questioning character. A diplomat and peacemaker with powerful emotions, although physical sensation is the chief function. A believer in personal enjoyment who seldom has regrets. Has an eye for beauty, is affectionate, and loves children and animals.

LIBRA

DISCOVERY — THIRD STEP

206°   *A hawk and a dove roost peacefully together*
A strong silent character. Very emotional, but thoughts take precedence. Displays a capacity for both peacemaking and aggression, but possesses a mischievous streak. Proud, self-confident and a good mixer. Usually generous, and likes to be thought a benefactor.

207°   *A small plane flies high in clear sky*
An independent, daring, ambitious character with a tremendous urge to achieve. Energetic, can be fierce and ruthless when opposed, but normally diplomatic. Tends to feel superior. Fond of high-living. Rejects second-best. Cares deeply for the family.

208°   *The man helped by the Good Samaritan*
A somewhat ambivalent character, emotional, but values logic highly. Likes to be thought firm-minded, but usually disorganized, No respecter of laws and customs. Sees through hypocrisy. A reliable judge of people, but tends to be over-critical.

209°   *A crowd of disciples eagerly follow their teacher*
An ardent character, always looking to the future. Highly emotional, and sensations are also very important. Trusting and eager to learn. Tends to follow fashion, but soon learns from experience. Sociable, keen to improve social status.

210°   *A palmist indicates a line denoting good fortune*
A realistic and sometimes fatalistic character, whose ambitions are always reaching out in a purposeful and optimistic manner. Firm-principled, often thought dogmatic and seldom listens to others' viewpoints. Tends to stand out in a crowd.

SCORPIO

MEMORY — FIRST STEP

211°   *A coach load of tourists crane their necks*
An eager, determined character with powerful emotions. Sociable, but introspective when alone. Has tendency to brood deeply and feel intensely. Likes to relax in calm surroundings when possible, but would love to be a leader. Possesses burning curiosity.

212°   *A discarded perfume bottle stills smells sweetly*
A thoughtful, dreamy character. Thoughts tend to be introverted, feelings extraverted. Sometimes seems broody, but happiest when alone. Fond of recalling memories. Cares little for morals. Somewhat temperamental and capable of losing temper.

213°   *A new building completed, the builders celebrate*
A confident, forward-looking character. Usually sociable and friendly. Thinking is the chief function along with powerful intuition. Emotions are inward-turned and private, so often thought unfeeling. Often alarmingly frank in criticizing others.

214°   *In church, children attend their confirmation service*
A rather serious thinking type with strong intuition. Has a great sense of self-worth. Self-confident, but always cautious at first in unfamiliar situations. Likes to be a group representative. Often a connoisseur of the arts. Very dependable.

215°   *An uninhabited shoreline, wild and rocky*
A cautious, somewhat severe character with a keen intellect. Tends to be lonely. The emotions are turned inwards which gives an impression of coldness. Hides worries in activity. Can be acquisitive but frugal. Suspicious of others' motives.

SCORPIO

MEMORY — SECOND STEP

216°   *Lured by gold, prospectors throng the wilderness*
A provident, resourceful character. A keen intellect mainly reserved
for work and material gain, deep emotions reserved for family and
inner needs. Adventurous, but makes wise use of resources. In
business a competitive opportunist.

217°   *Deep sea divers are lowered into the depths*
Powerful introverted emotions tend to take the place of rational
thought. Also makes good use of intuition. A candid person who
projects an air of innocence. Undemonstrative, and capable of great
sacrifices. Tolerant of others' shortcomings.

218°   *A moonlit lake in the mountains*
A brooding, strangely isolated character with great depth of
emotion. The mind tends to remain coldly rational. Imaginative,
likes to be thought practical. Can be moody and subject to fits of
temper. Often intensely ambitious and sometimes manipulative.

219°   *A dentist treats tooth decay in a child*
A zealous, restless character, very conscious of injustices.
Possesses great sympathy and tolerance for others' weaknesses.
Usually a jack-of-all-trades but often highly successful. Has great
stamina, and opposition only increases determination to succeed.

220°   *An emotional reunion of old comrades*
A persistently determined character. Thinking is the chief function,
with strong sensations. Practical, but can be sentimental at times.
Sociable and hard working, conscientious, reliable, usually bright
and cheerful.

SCORPIO

MEMORY — THIRD STEP

221°   *On the beach, a drowning man is rescued*
A sensitive, retiring character, usually a loner. Feelings are mainly turned inwards, thoughts outwards. Responsible, and can seem over-conscientious. Very loyal, but chooses few friends. Likes to be thought organized but often chaotic.

222°   *Government officials meet at an embassy ball*
An enthusiastic, ambitious character with a penetrating intellect. Tends to see life as a series of hurdles. Values material wealth highly, but likes to be thought of as possessing simple tastes. Even-tempered, usually conscientious, sometimes unscrupulous.

223°   *An inventor is busy in a back-room workshop*
An intense, punctilious character. Very versatile, conscientious and usually hard-working. Makes good use of intuition, but thoughts take precedence. Likes to appear sociable, but happiest when alone. Wears a happy face, but tends to brood in private.

224°   *Engineers establish a phone link across mountains*
An accomplished communicator with a keen brain and insatiable curiosity, forever probing and exploring. May go to great lengths to uncover facts, only to forget or discard them. A very physical person, usually with great stamina and energy.

225°   *Laughing children play on the sand dunes*
A lively, enthusiastic character. A sensation type whose emotions tend to be neglected; for this reason can seem unfeeling. Very sociable. Somewhat fatalistic, takes ups and downs of life lightly. Possesses a powerful drive for action, but readily becomes bored.

SCORPIO

VALUATION — FIRST STEP

226°   *A smiling girl with patrician features*
A calm, peaceful, thoughtful person. Loves influencing others and tends to be somewhat theatrical. Can use emotions to manipulate others. Hates aggression. Appears to treat matters lightly while taking them deeply to heart.

227°   *A pregnant woman, her face serene*
An alert character, eminently honest. Thinking is paramount but the emotions are powerful and outward-turned. Very sociable, friendly and tactful. Dislikes introspection. Capable of great achievements, but not very adaptable.

228°   *A winding track through autumn woods*
a penetrating, probing character, an explorer and experimenter. Has a keen intellect and uses intuition freely, but emotions tend to be neglected. Hates secrets, believing that both good and bad should be uncovered. May neglect family responsibilities.

229°   *A parrot repeats snatches of conversation*
A communicative, discursive character. Versatile but inconsistent, tends to begin projects only to abandon them. Often possesses a wide range of knowledge, tending to take details too seriously. Sociable, but enjoys own company too. Somewhat idiosyncratic.

230°   *A woman opens a white gate leading from the forest*
A thoughtful, reserved, modest character. Broad-minded, with deep emotions. Tends to take responsibilities too seriously. Hates to be pinned down and will change viewpoint rather than confront inflexibility. Affectionate, with strong family ties.

SCORPIO

VALUATION — SECOND STEP

231° *A young soldier goes absent to visit his wife*
A determined, versatile but somewhat reckless character. Emotional feelings tend to overrule logic, and life often seems chaotic, some may say quixotic. Possesses a firm code of conduct, but feels oppressed by regulations. Faithful but unpredictable.

232° *Wild-fowlers purposefully load their guns*
A self-assured, purposeful character. Possesses great energy, and usually the physical ability to use it to the full. A lover of challenges who can be brave and even ruthless in the face of opposition. Somewhat frugal in habits.

233° *Jack climbs the beanstalk and challenges the giant*
A modestly self-assured, conscientious, ever-hopeful character. Intuition comes to the fore, and emotions are kept firmly under control. Never temperamental. Determined not to surrender unless diplomacy demands it. Possesses great moral courage.

234° *Reassured, citizens leave a public enquiry*
An ardent, persistent, thrusting type. Intuitive, with a keenly penetrative mind. Seldom accepts anything at face value. Seldom completely open, but dislikes secrets in others. A self-analyzer, aware of own shortcomings and strives to overcome them.

235° *A doctor studies his patient's x-ray plates*
An earnest, diligent character with a great sense of duty. Tends to be lonely and always slightly aloof. Keenly analytical thoughts take precedence over the feelings. Feels need to discover the whole truth. Problems of others are taken seriously to heart.

SCORPIO

VALUATION — THIRD STEP

236°   *A nomadic tribe make their camp at dusk*
A prudent, well organized person, carefully prepared for all eventualities, seldom caught unawares. A resourceful provider. Thinking is the chief function but intuition is much used. Realistic, but sometimes prefers ideas over hard facts.

237°   *A full military band marches through the town*
A reflective, nostalgic character, more concerned with ideas than facts. Emotional feelings are uppermost, but when alone becomes very thoughtful. Likes to appear confident when in the public eye. A traditionalist happiest when working in a team.

238°   *King Oberon is greeted by Queen Titania*
A warmly sociable, apparently carefree character. Emotions are paramount, but the physical sensations are important. Sex impulses strong and uninhibited. Not given to introspection, Optimistic and positive, a staunch believer in equality.

239°   *A princess begs a conquering king to spare her sons*
A strangely wistful character, deeply emotional. Intuition seems to play a strong part in everyday life. Enjoys acting a role. Forever hoping for a better future but seldom really dissatisfied. Very sociable, tends to feel uneasy when alone.

240°   *Youngsters let off steam in an adventure playground*
An uninhibited character, often immoderate, with a great capacity for enjoyment. Physical sensations are all-important, and feelings are valued above logical thoughts. Not given to modesty and very inquisitive about other people. Always seeking new experiences.

SAGITTARIUS

DISCERNMENT — FIRST STEP

241°   *Red-coated army pensioners chat nostalgically*
A keenly perceptive, ruminative character. Very sociable and outgoing. Thinking is the chief psychological function, with powerful emotions. Tendency to mull over past events. A compulsive analyzer, sometimes over-involved with detail.

242°   *White crested waves leap as the wind freshens*
An earnest, ardent, active character, very sociable and extraverted. Highly emotional, takes causes strongly to heart. Sometimes thought self-centred. Tolerant of weakness in others. A formidable opponent, capable to going to great lengths.

243°   *Two old friends contentedly play chess*
A calmly self-confident character with a keen intellect and stable emotions. Sociable, but enjoys intimate circle best. Loves exploring the bounds of philosophical thought. Hard-working and expects the same of others. A lover of antiquity.

244°   *Encouraged by proud parents, a baby starts to walk*
A buoyant, optimistic, happily sociable character. Emotional feeling always takes precedence over logical thought but a great communicator. Hates the idea of loneliness and plans towards avoiding it. Family life may be neglected in favour of outsiders.

245°   *An old owl gazes down from a tree*
A gravely thoughtful intuitive type. Sensations introverted, leading to a vivid imagination. A good observer, curious, fond of analyzing motives. Often artistic. Sociable, quickly becoming bored with routine and likes to change familiar layouts.

SAGITTARIUS

DISCERNMENT — SECOND STEP

246°   *A cricket match with West Indian spectators*
An impetuous, fun-loving character. Physical sensations are all-important, with emotional feelings taking precedence over logic. Very sociable, tends to equate solitude with desolation. Usually very hard-working, truthful and conscientious.

247°   *Cupid aims his arrow at an unsuspecting heart*
An open and affectionate character. Often possesses a clever brain, but feelings and sensations take precedence. Sociable, with few self-doubts. Can seem erratic and irresponsible. Kind-hearted. Somewhat prone to infatuations. Often physically lazy.

248°   *Molten rock stirs in the centre of the earth*
An ambitious, determined character with a keen intellect. Regularly makes use of intuition to gain advantages. Possesses amazing vitality. Can seem immovably stubborn. Loves worthy causes. Enjoys luxury without luxuriating. Sociable, but happy when alone.

249°   *A mother helps her children up a long flight of stairs*
A restless visionary with an innovative turn of mind. Possesses deep feelings and a constructive imagination. Conscientious, energetic and responsible. Can be ruthless in pursuing objective. Sometimes aggressively over-defensive.

250°   *A speculator studies the latest share prices*
A bold and adventurous character fond of taking risks. Keen intellect, penetrating intuition, fiercely independent, a good provider. Dislikes boring routine. Often workaholic, forever seeking gain. Not averse to a little deception in business dealings.

SAGITTARIUS

DISCERNMENT — THIRD STEP

251°   *Seen by lantern light, an idol in an ancient temple*
A confident, unambiguous character with a great sense of tradition. Takes responsibilities gladly, but may tend to be dogmatic. Thinking and intuition always active, the emotions tend to become neglected. Loyal, unselfish, moral, a good provider.

252°   *A flag, an eagle, and a crowing cock*
A somewhat aggressive, confrontational type, bold and often physically brave. Sociable and extraverted, both thinking and feeling are to the fore. Often possesses a vast store of knowledge. Dislikes taking any new situation at face value.

253°   *A widow, still young, finds a new lover*
A restrained, almost repressive character. Values logical thinking and tends to scorn emotional reactions. Very sociable, seeming to avoid introspection. May seem uncaring to outsiders. Quietly confident and self-reliant. A keen debater.

254°   *The sphinx and pyramids stand in the desert*
A solidly self-assured character with few self-doubts. Thinking takes precedence over feeling, but intuition is much used to assess relationships. Likes to retain an air of mystery, intellectually if a male, and physically if female. A great communicator and traditionalist.

255°   *Swallows begin to gather on telephone wires*
A somewhat inflexible, idiosyncratic character. Very versatile. Powerful intuitions. Likes to be thought logical, but emotional feelings tend to overrule thought. Can be ruthless and stubborn. Seems to enjoy studying regulations, only to flout them.

SAGITTARIUS

FREEDOM — FIRST STEP

256° *A sailing ship is becalmed amid lazy seagulls*
A somewhat enigmatic, contemplative character. Sociable but quiet in company. Feelings are paramount, thoughts concerned more with passive than active images. Great capacity for close friendship. Often tardy, but critical of laziness in others.

257° *Druids await the dawn within a stone circle*
A great communicator with powerful intuition. Sociable, loves an audience. Tends to set great value on material possessions. Energetic in violent bursts. Tends towards extreme patterns of behaviour, but well-meaning. Welcomes serious responsibilities.

258° *Children wearing floppy hats play in the hot sun*
A somewhat possessive type, coolly rational, but also intuitive. Courageous when necessary but never reckless. Always seems friendly, but tends to feel isolated. Can be very proud, with great confidence in own ability. May adopt extravagant ways.

259° *On a lonely lake, wild birds take to the wing*
Earnest and studious, a thinker with creative imagination. Likes to claim a retiring nature, but enjoys the social whirl. Versatile, will apply great energy only to change course suddenly. Likes to be thought sophisticated.

260° *After the harvest, a farmer begins ploughing afresh*
A resolute, enterprising character, with tremendous stamina. Loves trying out new theories but never dismayed by boring routine. Takes responsibilities seriously. Sometimes follows new enterprises recklessnessly. Happy in company or alone.

SAGITTARIUS

FREEDOM — SECOND STEP

261°   *A boy and his dog play with a ball*
An uneasy character, sincere but impetuous. Powerful emotions. Great energy, often channelled fiercely. Can be unpredictable and difficult to live with, but enjoys team efforts. Often righteously indignant.

262°   *After a battle, soldiers relax and play cards*
A confident and purposeful character. Sensations take precedence over the other functions, and emotions are often neglected. Friendly and sociable within own circle, very family-orientated, but aggressive towards outsiders.

263°   *The pilgrim fathers land in the New World*
An adventurous, proud, forceful character. Thinking takes precedence, but very physical and practical. Seldom given to self-doubt, tending to feel superior to most. Seldom admits defeat. Can seem pious, but is rarely humble. Not given to amusements.

264°   *The blue bird of happiness perches on a cottage roof*
A genial, happy, trustful, warmly emotional type. Sensation usually takes priority over thoughts. Optimistic, can seem exasperatingly complacent. Creatively imaginative. A great home-lover with few material ambitions or needs.

265°   *A smartly dressed girl rides her favourite pony*
A confident, self-controlled character, psychologically well-balanced. Tends to play down talents. Possesses a gently superior attitude. Tactful, but can be scathing when thought necessary. A lover of luxury, but seldom to the point of extravagance.

SAGITTARIUS

FREEDOM— THIRD STEP

266°   *A standard bearer distinguishes himself in battle*
A well-intentioned character who usually seems to be following a different agenda to anyone else. Strongly intuitive and emotional. Socially confident. Imaginative and artistically inclined. Romantic, but can become bad-tempered.

267°   *A statue takes shape beneath the sculptor's hand*
A practical, ambitious, inventive character. Socially confident. Always seems to be in a hurry, and likes to be seen as self-made. Often feels like an outsider. Needs close family ties and exclusive circle of friends. Possesses a great sense of physical beauty.

268°   *An ancient Roman aqueduct is still in daily use*
A staunchly reliable, eminently practical character. Intuitive and emotional. Often sees possibilities overlooked by more highly intelligent people. Ambitious, often in unconventional directions. Confident in company. Likes to come straight to the point.

269°   *A stout lady works energetically, trying to lose weight*
An earnest, dedicated type, powerfully emotional, strongly physical, outgoing and energetic. Takes responsibilities seriously. Usually cheerfully reliable, but hates being taken for granted. Enjoys small luxuries and the security of familiar routines.

270°   *The Pope is holding audience in the Vatican*
A dignified and rather solemn character. Thoughtful, with emotions somewhat inward-turned. Always ready to take responsibility. Possesses a genuine liking for people but can besharply critical. Feels a strong need for material security.

CAPRICORN

WONDER — FIRST STEP

271°   *At a board meeting, a new chairman is appointed*
A bold, energetic, innovative character. A deep thinker and often a talented all-rounder. Sociable and self-assured. Responsible. Prefers to seek general approval before taking action. Frequently displays magnetic charm.

272°   *a stained glass window in a bombed cathedral*
A sensitive, emotional individualist with a great sense of duty. A perfectionist who tends to be over-critical. Sometimes touchy. Takes injustices to heart. Unselfish. Recovers quickly from mishaps. sometimes expresses the wish to conform and be one of the crowd.

273°   *A white dove circles high above*
An uneasy character, emotional and somewhat introverted. Tends to be a dreamer rather than a doer, preferring ideas to facts. Likes to be seen as dynamic, and often ends up facing opposition and fighting against the odds. Can be over-critical.

274°   *Party goers take a boat ride on the lake*
A fervent, somewhat ruthless character. Often a strict disciplinarian. Usually attached emotionally to one particular social circle. Sensual pleasures play an important role in life. Faithful in intent, but not always in practice. Sometimes over-fond of luxury.

275°   *Children learn warfare in a Third World village*
An impulsive person, hot-headed and venturesome, but highly principled. Uses intuition freely when dealing with others. Tends to make enemies. Believes in rightness of own cause. Loves stirring others out of complacency.

120

CAPRICORN

WONDER — SECOND STEP

276°   *A pioneer gazes across a valley at new virgin forests*
An intense, inventive type. Eminently practical thinker, hard working, always looking ahead and striving for success. Altruistic, with lofty ideals and down-to-earth thoughts. Values performance over preaching. Can be short-tempered.

277°   *A committee decides on a firm course of action*
An uncompromising, resolutely logical type. Feels things deeply but rarely expresses feelings openly. Possesses powerful capacity for intuition. Highly principled but can seem unscrupulous. Tends to change direction often for an equally uncompromising course.

278°   *A sleeping cat and a canary in a luxurious room*
A peaceful, pensive character. Emotional function paramount, but rarely expressed openly. Affectionate, loyal, usually gentle and even-tempered, but capable of violent action if really aroused. When relaxed can seem frivolous.

279°   *A country curate peacefully tends his garden*
A sentimental character given to reminiscence. Possesses a keen intellect and equally powerful emotions. Sociable and a keen social observer, but needs a private retreat. Tends to moralize, but aims at impartiality. Projects an air of innocent superiority.

280°   *Old time sailors throw food to a circling albatross*
A discreet, cautious, circumspect character. Thinking takes precedence, but tends to be introverted. Practical, conscientious, accurate, diplomatic, conservative. Tends to be suspicious of strangers and new ideas. Aims to eliminate possible risks.

CAPRICORN

WONDER — THIRD STEP

281°   *Golden pheasants feed near a stately home*
A capricious character. Often possesses an acute mind. Sociable and enjoys being the centre of attention but likes to feel separate from the herd. Enjoys joking about the faults of others whilst ignoring own shortcomings. Generous however, and fairly highly principled.

282°   *A television documentary on natural science*
A thoughtful person with an enquiring mind. Versatile, energetic. Loves mysteries but dislikes secrets. Sex impulses powerful and pure. Likes to adopt an air of judicial ignorance when listening to others. May indulge in innocent gossip.

283°   *A fakir sits alone on a Himalayan mountain*
An earnest, dedicated and somewhat isolated character. Possesses powerful capacity for sensations and a vivid imagination. Not very sociable, enjoys own company in peace. Self-critical, but patient with others' faults. Conscientious but sometimes lazy.

284°   *The tomb of a Pharaoh, as yet unplundered*
A somewhat idiosyncratic character, with a keen thinking mind turned inwards, and powerful emotions turned outwards. Possesses a vivid imagination and an eye for beauty and symbolism. Often pursues unusual knowledge.

285°   *A children's hospital ward, well stocked with toys*
A warmly lavish character. Likes to be seen as a provider. Very sensitive to others' needs and ready to help. Feelings take precedence over thoughts. Energetic and practical. Tends to be critical of others' morals. Often addicted to small luxuries.

CAPRICORN

DEPENDENCE — FIRST STEP

286° *A school gymnasium, buzzing with activity*
An exuberant person. Very practical with a keen intellect. A good team member, but sociable as a duty rather than a pleasure. Conscientious, hard-working, helpful person who dislikes slackers. Values security highly.

287° *On the beach, a woman removes her costume top*
A strangely wistful character. A keen observer of people, but keeps observations private. Would like to be less inhibited. Sometimes seems to prefer strangers to family. Tends to commence new ventures only to abandon them. Very sympathetic with weaknesses.

288° *A warship flying the flag on her maiden voyage*
A quietly confident type. Thinking takes precedence, and emotions directed chiefly towards own family circle. Highly perceptive of the motives of others. Can be cold and calculating, and ruthless when security is threatened. Brave and self-controlled.

289° *A child dutifully helps mother with the shopping*
A determined character with a keen intellect. Sensations are important and usually turned inward, resulting in a vivid imagination. Adaptable, unimpressed by surroundings. Tolerant of friends, but tends to be critical of outsiders.

290° *Choir practice is taking place in church*
A calm and well-adjusted person. Emotional feelings take precedence over thinking. Self-sufficient, but enjoys company. Likes to be seen as easy-going, but possesses fairly strict morals. Sensitive to atmosphere. Kind hearted in a gently superior way.

CAPRICORN

DEPENDENCE — SECOND STEP

291° *Before a relay race, team members limber up*
A determined, venturesome character. Thinking takes precedence, with almost equally powerful feelings. Possesses strong powers of persuasion, with faith in own ability and judgment. Enjoys the limelight and likes to stand out as a leader. Rarely relaxes.

292° *A defeated general hands over his sword with dignity*
A gentle, affectionate, submissive character. Functions of thinking and sensation both turned inward. Powerful animal instincts. An optimist, Prefers imaginative ideas over facts. Enjoys simple pleasures. Hates quarrels and confrontation.

293° *A soldier is twice decorated for bravery*
A thrusting, masterful type who takes responsibilities seriously. Loves to be the leader. Highly emotional. Can readily become depressed if under-rated. Usually highly moral, physically daring, rarely modest. A doer who tends not to learn from experience.

294° *A woman thankfully enters a convent*
An individualistic, dedicated character. Thinking takes precedence over emotions which are inward-turned. Intuitive, helpful and kind when required. Cares deeply but often seems cold. Often thought eccentric. Tends to pursue unusual causes adventurously.

295° *Little boys play on rich oriental carpets*
A quietly confident character. Sociable, but always feels apart from the crowd. Tends to take self too seriously. Possesses an air of innocence with few self-doubts. Responsible. Fond of luxury. Always looking for deep meanings in everyday situations.

CAPRICORN

DEPENDENCE — THIRD STEP

296°   *A luminous sprite dances on the mist of a waterfall*
A buoyant, flexible character. Thinking takes precedence but is turned inwards. Interested in ideas rather than facts. Undemonstrative. Indecisive in social issues but boldly decisive in pursuing enterprise. Responsible. Often displays unusual knowledge.

297°   *On the summit of Everest the climbers meditate*
A resolute character, one of the most outgoing of Capricornians. Possesses great energy. Often physical and can be aggressive. Will try again and again to ensure success. Always practical. Often outwardly religious but inwardly self-dependent.

298°   *In a privately-owned aviary the birds are singing*
An uncompromisingly earnest character. Emotional feelings take precedence over logical thoughts. Seldom feels self-doubt. Somewhat iconoclastic, but always well-meaning. Can be fiercely critical and ignore others' feelings.

299°   *A gipsy reads tealeaves in an opulent drawing room*
An irrepressibly vivacious character. Usually outgoing. Emotional feelings warm but thoughts cold and logical. Intuition much used but largely inward-turned. Dislikes being alone. Seems oddly divided between vice and virtue.

300°   *The board of directors call a secret meeting*
A prudent, serious character. Thinking takes precedence. Emotions are strong but seldom expressed openly. Affectionate but undemonstrative. Never acts before taking careful thought. A very private person, sometimes seems complacent.

AQUARIUS

CONSERVATION — FIRST STEP

301°   *An old ancestral home in the hills*
A thrusting, compulsive, masterful character with a practical, enquiring mind. Often comes up with good ideas. Very energetic. Possesses great curiosity about people and places. Very sociable and hates solitude.

302°   *A long awaited thunder storm breaks*
A dramatic, tempestuous character. Possesses a vivid imagination and an astute mind. Forever seeing familiar events in a new way. Much given to nostalgia. Loves to travel. Lives energetically and may overtax physical strength. Gregarious and talkative.

303°   *A fugitive resolves to return to society*
A strangely wistful, yearning character. Tends to keep others at arm's length while longing for intimate company. Emotional feeling takes precedence over logical thought, but feelings rather inward-turned. Frequently suffers from vague feelings of guilt.

304°   *A man discovers that he has the gift of healing*
A self-assured, somewhat unadaptable character. Strongly emotional, kind-hearted and sociable.harbours few self-doubts. Likes the idea of helping others, but tends to suspect the worst in people and can become critical and short-tempered.

305°   *An ornate clock is a family heirloom*
A determined, resourceful character. Thinking takes precedence over feeling, but the emotionstoo are powerful. Sensuous and sociable, but with few close friends. Always keeps part of self private. Feels obligations very strongly.

AQUARIUS

CONSERVATION — SECOND STEP

306°   *A parish priest conducts a simple service alone*
An independent, self-sufficient character. Thinking takes precedence over feelings, with strongly developed intuition. Very sociable, but enjoys own company too. Likes to be relied upon to take responsibility and organize everything.

307°   *A new-born baby is sleeping on a white blanket*
An earnest character with an oddly direct simplicity of purpose. Often extremely talented, energetic and productive. Highly intuitive. Very observant. May tend to over-specialize and become obsessive. Feels affection but rarely respect for others.

308°   *Smartly dressed dummies in a shop window*
A very emotional type, somewhat brash and forceful. Unpredictable. A great individualist, very inventive. Feels keen need for luxury and bodily comforts. Usually pays great attention to personal appearance. A confident debater, with great nervous energy.

309°   *A fierce eagle perches on a flag pole*
A determined, somewhat eccentric character. Emotional feelings take precedence over logic, but still capable of prolonged concentration. Carries an air of proud authority. Likes to be seen as a provider, and is often to be found in areas of hardship.

310°   *A once well known performer stages a come-back*
Sentimental, responsive, affectionate and romantic, a rather unadaptable person who tends to dwell on past errors and triumphs. Emotional feeling is always to the fore. Always nostalgic for the past and hopeful for the future.

AQUARIUS

CONSERVATION — THIRD STEP

311°   *A reclusive artist commits an inspiration to canvas*
A creatively imaginative person. The function of sensation is powerful and introverted, emotions powerful and extraverted. Has great feeling for natural beauty. Enjoys taking chances, but feels a deep and private need for security. Quiet but with noisy outbursts.

312°   *A* broad *stairway has successive landings*
A systematic, prudent character. Ambitious, friendly, diplomatic, quite highly intuitive, but one who likes to keep real feelings private. Enjoys taking charge of situations, and always takes responsibility for mishaps. A natural planner and forecaster.

313°   *A quiet country inn with a barometer in the porch*
A quietly resourceful, practical, inventive type. Thinking takes precedence but has warm emotional feelings and a powerful imagination. Enjoys being the brains behind the scenes. Likes solitude but is rarely reclusive.

314°   *A mountain pass is driven through a tunnel*
A versatile, enquiring character, inquisitive, with a talent for discovering facts, but always slow to give out information. Always realistic, tends to be materialistic, always seeking rational explanations. Emotions inward-turned and rarely expressed.

315°   *Young children play happily in an old churchyard*
An exuberantly enthusiastic person with powerful physical sensations. Capable of keen thought and prolonged concentration. Very sociable, loves new experiences, and tends to be hedonistic. Dislikes social restraints, and can seem irresponsible.

AQUARIUS

ANTICIPATION — FIRST STEP

316°   *The managing director studies a complex report*
A natural diplomat with an analytical turn of mind. Intuitive, thoughtful and well-intentioned. Emotional feelings tend to be under-used. Optimistic, responsible, likes to think the best of people. Values frankness and dislikes secrets and hidden feelings.

317°   *A guard dog remains alert while its master sleeps*
A fearlessly confident character. Thinking and intuition are jointly prominent. Possesses tremendous stamina. Loves positions of authority. Has a sincere desire to do good, but needs to feel admired. Usually friendly, but can be aggressive if necessary.

318°   *At a masked ball the final guest unmasks*
An observant, somewhat romantic explorer. Thinking takes precedence, with intuition much used. Possesses a vivid imagination. Affectionate and sociable, but enjoys puncturing pomposity in others. Likes to be thought systematic.

319°   *The fire extinguished, weary firemen celebrate*
A very sociable character with a great capacity for hard work and enjoyment. Extraverted thinking function, with emotions well under control. Conscientious, enjoys public service. Tends to be depressed when feeling isolated.

320°   *A white dove circles a house, then lands on the roof*
One of the most peace-loving and patient of Aquarians. Emotional. Tends to neglect physical sensations and health. Not very sociable, but dislikes solitude. Optimistic. Usually reliable, but capable of changing viewpoint easily. Not too concerned with details.

AQUARIUS

ANTICIPATION — SECOND STEP

321°   *A woman is disappointed as a man leaves*
A highly emotional, somewhat eccentric character. Sometimes appears to reject reasoned argument in favour of sentiment. Usually affectionate and capable of great self-sacrifice. Sociable but with few close friends. Becomes short-tempered when feeling guilty.

322°   *Babies crawl and play on a soft new carpet*
A strangely contradictory character. Very determined, eminently physical, with keen, aggressive modes of thought. Great self-assurance, often ambitious, can seem obstinate and ruthless, but at the same time oddly innocent. Tends to brood darkly.

323°   *A huge circus bear balances on a barrel*
An unselfish, kindly but ambitious character. A true extravert, diplomatic and strongly principled, capable of outstanding achievements. Always looking for ways of improving the life situation, often with the aim of climbing socially. Possesses keen powers of reasoning.

324°   *Freed from repression, a teacher discovers wisdom*
An independent intellectual explorer with keen powers of observation. A natural analyst, capable of great concentration. Emotional feelings tend to become neglected. Dislikes popular, conventional pursuits, and seldom takes things for granted.

325°   *A hatching chick is emerging from the eggshell*
An eager, venturesome character. A thinking type, often using the power of intuition. Sometimes seems to possess a sixth sense. Emotional feelings turned inward. Tenacious and inquisitive, more interested in problems than in people.

AQUARIUS

ANTICIPATION — THIRD STEP

326°   *A car battery is being recharged at a power-point*
A temperamental and highly emotional character. Although feelings tend to be impractical, thinking is always down-to-earth. Passionate, with outbursts of temper. Capable of tremendous energy, but quite able to remain passive for long periods.

327°   *Old books, an antique vase, and fresh violets*
A broad-minded, persuasive character who loves to be the source of enlightenment. Reliable, always optimistic. Likes to represent some special organization or class of people. Never flippant. May sometimes miscalculate others' feelings and seem overbearing.

328°   *Firewood is stacked ready for winter*
A caring, warmly emotional character. Practical, with a clever mind, but tends to waste serious efforts through unrestrained imagination. Usually happily sociable with a genuine love for people. May be untidy, with a tendency to hoard.

329°   *A dragonfly, newly emerged from the pond*
A pensive person, highly intuitive and somewhat self-conscious. Emotional feelings take precedence over logical thought. Introspective, often seeming withdrawn and somewhat eccentric. Sometimes talkative. Usually optimistic.

330°   *Bare moonlit fields where an ancient city once stood*
A serenely confident character. A thinking type, with powerful physical sensations. Highly sociable. A very proud person with few self-doubts. Energetic, can seem boisterous at times and aggressive, but never malicious. Marital life tends to be turbulent.

PISCES

HOPE — FIRST STEP

331°   *A supermarket is busier than ever on Saturday night*
A friendly, bustling type. Very sociable, yet can be introspective. Feelings tend to be reserved for the nearest and dearest. Sincere and honest, but with a tendency to exaggerate. Loves to reminisce. Needs to belong to an organized group.

332°   *Well camouflaged, a solder keeps watch*
An active crusader, often strongly physical. The function of sensation takes precedence, with powerful emotional feelings. Can be ruthless. Patient until the moment for action arrives. Can remain calm in a crisis. Enjoys being in the public eye.

333°   *In the desert stands an ancient ruined city*
A coolly self-assured type, often intellectually inclined. Emotional feelings tend to be neglected. Possesses few self-doubts. Rather introverted but seldom shy. Kindly, determined and courageous if need be. Usually seen as practical and dependable.

334°   *An express train is crowded with passengers*
A communicator, one of the most outgoing of Pisceans. Eminently sociable, even tempere,d and warm of feeling for others. Hates solitude. Versatile, competitive, eager to learn. A traditionalist who dislikes secrets. Very observant.

335°   *Supporters throng the stalls at a bring-and-buy sale*
A philosophical character with a vivid imagination. Thinking is paramount and mainly turned inward. Possesses a burning curiosity, and loves to examine motives and beliefs. Often thought frivolous, but deeply serious inside.

PISCES

HOPE — SECOND STEP

336°   *Army recruits are on parade as the sun sets*
A daringly competitive, dedicated character, intuitive and often very physical. Emotional feelings are paramount. Very energetic, sometimes taking pleasure in aggression, but usually fun-loving. Sociable, and takes pride in belonging to a group.

337°   *Fog shrouds the shore, but a guiding light gleams*
A contented, self-possessed, confident character with a deep inward faith. Often appears aimless or even confused to others who see only the surface appearance. Capable of great love and sacrifice, readily forming attachments.

338°   *An exuberant bugle call sounds in a scout camp*
An ambitious, enthusiastic character. Thinking is the chief function, with powerful intuition. Wears an air of determination. Works and plays hard. Makes a valued and versatile leader. Can be very stubborn or ruthless as a youth, mellowing later.

339°   *A jockey is riding in the big race*
A dogged individualist capable of immense effort. Often thought eccentric. Often becomes attached to some special cause or school of thought. Likes to stand out from the crowd and dislikes holding popular opinions. Affectionate only within an intimate circle.

340°   *A hot air balloon floats clear of the trees*
An independent adventurer, intuitive, with a keen brain. One who makes wise judgments, but often mars them with precipitous action. Ambitious, energetic, but capable of instant relaxation. Unpredictable, but usually gets results.

PISCES

HOPE — THIRD STEP

341°   *Pilgrims arrive at a sacred shrine*
An eager, bustling person. Frank, conscientious, sometimes over-punctilious, highly practical, open-hearted, hard working, versatile. Can become frustrated when plans do not proceed as hoped. Sometimes irritable. Prefers own company for relaxation.

342°   *University students sit their final exam*
A somewhat uneasy character, usually possessing a keen brain. Feelings too are strong and largely introverted. Tends to lack self-confidence and fall short of own expectations, which causes anguish. Strongly principled. Helpful but often misunderstood.

343°   *A museum case contains a ceremonial sword*
A dignified character, calm on the surface but often in turmoil within. Possesses a powerful emotional attachment to the past, whilst thoughts tend to dwell on future possibilities. Very independent and dedicated, often specializing deeply and seriously.

344°   *A glamorous girl is clad in mink*
A self-confident, somewhat ostentatious character. A thinker with a keen brain. Very extraverted with a real need to communicate freely. Precise and realistic. If male, is proud of knowledge and skills. If female, is proud of appearance and possessions.

345°   *A commando officer blackens his face*
A somewhat repressive type, forever holding natural impulses in check. Emotional feelings take precedence. Likes to be seen as carefree, but in fact conscientious and law-abiding. Can be ruthless. Capable of prolonged efforts.

PISCES

REASSURANCE — FIRST STEP

346°   *An art student sits quietly in a museum*
A reflective, conscientious character. Thinking takes precedence, with a keen brain. Emotional feelings are used mainly to persuade others. Capable of arguing with passionate conviction. Industrious, peaceful and versatile.

347°   *Villagers walk to church in their Sunday best*
A receptive, impressionable character, dedicated to improvement. Always tries to champion the underdog. Dislikes unorthodox opinions and cares greatly for old things, rites and customs. Great appetite for learning. Self-critical but patient with others.

348°   *A well known revivalist conducts a mass crusade*
An emotional communicator. Intuitive, tends to belittle generally accepted values. Materially generous. Kindly, but projects an air of superiority. Dislikes secrets and hidden agendas. Not very realistic, tending to ignore inconvenient facts. Helpful when help is needed.

349°   *A party of school children on a practical project*
A sincerely dedicated, industrious type. Thinking takes precedence, but emotions run calm and deep. Will work patiently with a group, but at best when achieving through individual effort. Persistent and thorough. Sociable, but also values solitude.

350°   *A farmer goes home for his supper*
A resolute, well balanced character. energetic, capable of facing hardship without complaint, but greatly appreciative of luxuries. Versatile. Enjoys an element of risk. Needs a faithful partner, and at best when self-employed.

PISCES

REASSURANCE — SECOND STEP

351°　*A young girl trains her pony*
A lively, intense, highly physical character with powerful sensations. Often very imaginative. Has a great sense of fun, but there is a repressively strict side to the personality. Tends to be a loner in youth, becoming more sociable and affectionate in later years.

352°　*An industrialist speaks at a business convention*
A contradictory character, hopeful but constantly frustrated. Thoughtful and ambitious, but plans seem rarely to come to fruition. Sociable and friendly with a powerful imagination. Tends to be somewhat lazy when vigorous action is called for, and *vice versa.*

353°　*A conjuror performs amazing tricks*
A resolute achiever. Thinking takes precedence, with powerful use of intuition. Possesses a vivid imagination and the ability to put ideas into practice. Ambitious, aiming to discover new fields of endeavour, physical and mental. Seldom openly affectionate.

354°　*A family of castaways optimistically build a shelter*
A confidently enthusiastic type. Emotional feeling takes precedence over thoughts, which tend towards introversion. Capable of working hard, but often appears impractical or idealistic. Easy-going, adaptable, not particularly sociable but usually well liked.

355°　*Chastened, a reformed delinquent starts a new life*
A prudent, realistic, somewhat deferential character. Tends towards introversion, but emotional feelings are largely directed outwards. Tends to suffer from feelings of guilt. Full of theories and novel ideas. Reliable, and affectionate.

PISCES

REASSURANCE — THIRD STEP

356°   *Two lovers and a philosopher gaze at the full moon*
An enthusiastic character, inveterately romantic. Thinking and feeling are well balanced. Largely an introverted intuitive type. Tends to see deep meanings in almost any situation. Possesses a keen eye for natural beauty. Capable of great efforts.

357°   *A red moon silhouettes the falling leaves of autumn*
A wistful character with an air of sadness. Emotional and rather introverted. Optimistic, even in the face of overwhelming odds. Shyness leads to the adoption of haughty mannerisms. Romantic but realistic. Conscientious. Often talented artistically.

358°   *Seen by moonlight, the countryside looks different*
An innovative, thoughtful, emotionally stable character. Much given to pensive recapitulation. Tends to enjoy repetitive humour, despite originality of thought. Sociable and confident, reliable,conscientious, often talented artistically.

359°   *Scientific analysis is being carried out by computer*
A very thorough, dedicated character. Usually possesses a very keen brain. Takes pride in remaining calm in emergencies. Capable of great energy. Often suffers from unexplained feelings of guilt. Can seem pernickety, and home life tends to be chaotic.

360°   *A giant face has been carved into a mountain*
A serenely self-assured character. Well balanced, usually successful, and likes to be thought a person of solid achievement. Seldom selfish, but values material attainment very highly. Dependable, proud, but seldom feels superior.

CHAPTER 5

Evolution and personal choice

Manifestly, the sequence of degree symbols can be seen as a sequence of phases of self-building. They are like the notes of an as yet unwritten human symphony. The majority of people live fragmented and comparatively unfulfilled lives, making use of only a tiny part of their potential selves. Zodiac degree symbolism, in forming collective pictures, can suggest the nature of potential *dharma,* and pinpoint the chance of new growth for the individual.

Because one's exact birth time is rarely known accurately it is no use being too dogmatic about the selection of a symbol in relation to the ascendant degree and its angular relationships when interpreting a birth chart. The significance of each symbol — of each degree — is released the moment it begins, and there is no hangover period. But this is no real problem; intuition will often indicate the appropriate degree from any set of five. But because the symbols arise from and refer to the essence of *collective* awareness, they can in any case most confidently be applied to the Sun sign, and the "collective" outer planets.

The framework of the inner self, as we have seen, is formed of collective rather than personal elements, though actual soul contents are personal to each individual. In this sense all are one, for "soul contents" are not permanent acquisitions; they are mutable. The collective realm must be the chief source of clues to individual development, to rebirth in the spiritual sense.

Every part of the non-polar Earth is bathed in the Sun's light over its whole surface about 365 times a year, and yet there

138

are only 360 degrees with which to record the fact, and apparently only 360 basic human "types" according to the degree symbols. A further spiritual dimension to a degree is hinted at by the fact that, when the average number of days in the year — 365.2 — is divided by 360 it leaves a remainder of 0.014. This is said to be the cabbalistic "mysterious fourteen" latent within every day and every degree — the factor by which we are said to be able to grow culturally and evolve spiritually each year; our coming to the puberty of creative awareness. Nothing in the planetary sense is fixed and static, and the factor of fourteen can symbolize the difference between rigidity and flexibility.

In our context the mysterious fourteen may be taken to represent the difference between form and spirit, between unreasoning adherence to arbitrary law, and the freedom of wisdom. Without this inbuilt room for development it would not be possible for us to progress beyond spiritual ignorance and the bondage of fate. Symbolically, it allows for evolution, for change, for free will, leading eventually to submission to the divine will. It is a symbol of hope that human spiritual aspiration will not go unrewarded. In both the individual and the collective spheres, the potentiality exists for us to escape the influence of the zodiac, through a gradual but steady process of psychic maturity and spiritual growth.

Early Christians noted the fourteen year span of development on a grander scale: the Jewish people took their ancestral descent very seriously, and St Matthew's Gospel records that there were fourteen generations from Abraham to King David, fourteen generations from David to the period of exile in Babylon, and fourteen generations from Babylon to the coming of Christ. A sequence, that is, of fourteen from the original instinctive awareness of spirituality, as yet uncivilized, to the state of stability symbolized by the Judean dynasty; a sequence of fourteen to the loss of freedom and the fate of religious superstition; a sequence of fourteen from this captivity to the possibility of wisdom and spiritual renewal.

Axial rotation of the Earth, as registered by the ascendant degree of the birth chart, certainly represents a process of self development, of increasing awareness, and this process requires a measure of introspection, a looking-inwards in the old, self-centred way. But the greater orbital movement of the Earth implies a shift in the centre of self and a movement towards the purifying realm of the collective unconscious. We know that the birth chart horizon represents the division, not only between day and night, but also between conscious and unconscious, between objective and subjective. Meridian, on the other hand, could be said to represent the pendulum of karma; in separating sunrise from sunset it divides cause and effect, giving out and taking in, power and submission.

This is the traditional geocentric view. But the heliocentric view is best taken, for a while at least, when the inner self is under consideration. Symbolically, in this case, the Sun is always standing, as it were, at mid-heaven, surrounded by the multiple whirling components of the potentially integrated life-principle which it represents. If anything symbolized within astrology could be said to be imposed upon the individual at birth, it is surely the collective character focused through the zodiac degree of the Sun sign. This never-setting Sun of the collective inner self may be visualized as standing permanently at the objective zenith of the birth chart meridian.

When seen in this way, as a simplified alternative to the standard method of erecting a chart, the appropriate degree and its three angular correspondents can be used to produce a meaningful character sketch at a deep level — at that level of character, shall we say, that exists at birth before the childhood development of the conventional personality, before the sophisticated complications of logical thinking, emotional feeling and physical experience have played their part.

The diagram opposite should be seen as a continuous cycle, a constantly interacting stream of influences stemming from and working upon each other, symbolized entirely by the word

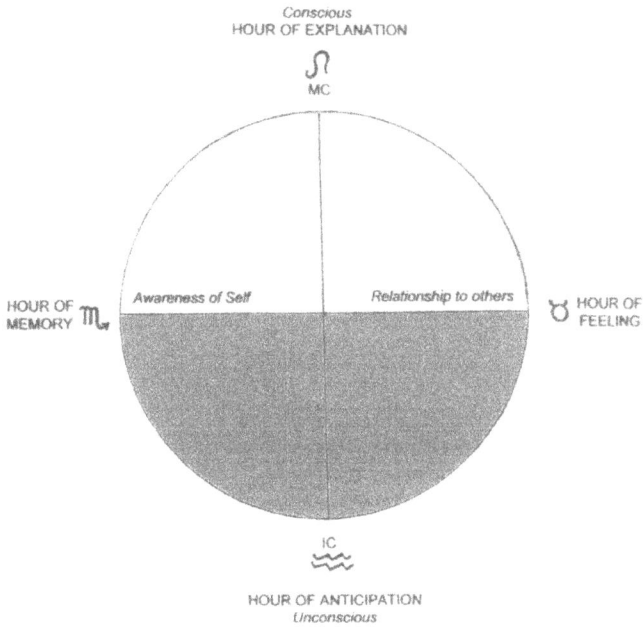

A Character Sketch

pictures associated with the relevant degrees. The Sun degree represents the cardinal point of potential *libido,* the uninhibited goal of all striving within the collective zone of human spirituality. Thepolarity of this Sun degree will then represent the subjective side of the soul-personality, a potentially modifying, cooling influence which operates beneath the threshold of awareness. This subjective degree representing the developing personal unconscious has the effect of balancing the whole evolving personality. It could be identified with Jung's *shadow,* a collection of unrealized urges gradually assembled from unconsciously creative sources. The growth of this psychic shadow along with the

141

developing personality depends largely upon environment and opportunity. Open to the soul but closed to the mind, the shadow is neither good not bad. Though certainly no more "spiritual" than other aspects of the self, it often seems to have a religious flavour, because its later recognition and conscious acceptance as part of the whole self is a necessary precondition for spiritual development.

Now, in this simplified diagram of the undeveloped self, the ascendant at 90° on from the objectivity of the Sun degree, may be said to relate to the developing ego in the commonly accepted sense of the word. At the point of balance between objectivity abd subjectivity, it expresses the individual potential sense of selfhood, the way in which he or she is destined habitually to view the outside world. In taking the place of the birth chart ascendant degree, it represents the newborn infant starting out in life, the birth of *calculated* will.

The degree directly opposed to this "soul ascendant" now relates to *submissive relationships,* a cryptic side to the character of a new soul as yet uninfluenced by the surrounding world. Its associate word picture suggests the potentially developing nature of a "spiritual personality", as a culmination of the other three principles present at birth. Each cardinal point within this personal but at the same time collective mandala, as in the birth chart proper, registers a culmination or product of its associate degrees working in a continuous cycle. They indicate how powerful is the part being played by the inner feelings in determining how the subject will experience physical life on Earth. As there is no real beginning or ending to a circle, it indicates too how the self at the deep level of soul has already been formed and is full of content, even at the moment of birth.

Character analysis

Having ascertained these "psychic angles", the degree symbols may be applied to provide a character analysis expressive of the "soul nature". Let me take as an example, and with his permission, my friend David Oliver, a fellow astrologer and spiritual seeker whose interesting birth chart is analyzed in Chapter 7. At his birth the Sun registered the final degree of Gemini. Using this system, his objective degree will be 90°, the corresponding subjective degree will be 270°. On the horizon the degree representing his ascendant will be 180°, with 360° indicating his descendant.

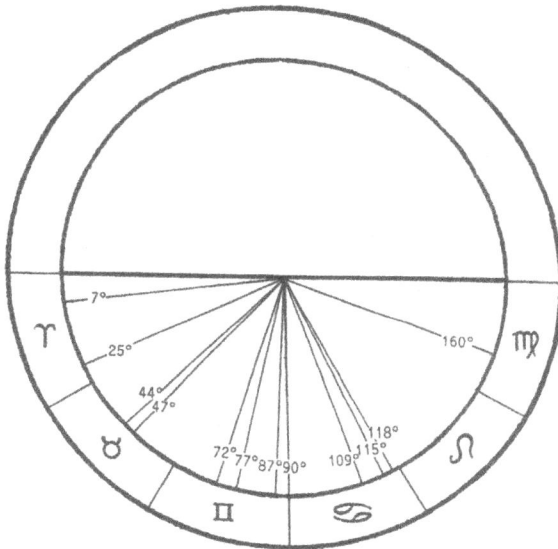

The Split or "Schizoid" Degrees

A few zodiac degree symbols seem to include the quality of duality within their significance, and 90° is one of these. Other examples are: 7°, 25°, 44°, 47°, 72°, 77°, 87°, 109°, 115°, 118°, and 160°. When set against the dial of mundane houses — that is, the chart of the soul — these twelve degrees will be seen to be limited to the lower half of the chart, normally relating to "selfhood", the subjective areas of intuition and feeling. Individuals

ASTROLOGY AND THE INNER SELF

in whose birth chart one or more of these dual degrees feature strongly seem to be more aware than most of their own underlying nature, do not care to be made to conceal it for whatever social reasons, and when forced to do so may react oddly. We have already borrowed Jung's terms to describe the psychic angles; to borrow another of his terms, we can say that these symbols hint at the nature of an "introverted feeling" type, or equally, an "introverted intuitive" type. They may refer to what Jung described as the "schizoid" personality.

The symbol for 90° is: *A beauty contest is being held on the beach.* The dual quality of this symbol can readily be seen: the essence of a beauty contest is to segregate the sexes — or, at least, the comely from the homely — and then to allow the one division to judge the other. Not only that; the section about to be judged, in the manner of beauty contestants, is going to be equally critical in judging itself. There is continual opposition between judging, and being judged. This is typical of a split or "schizoid" degree.

This individual is bound to be sensitive about what people think of him. He plays a dual role: when he feels himself to be under judgment he will be very conscientious, and painfully honest about his shortcomings; and when acting as judge himself he may be fiercely critical of others, though usually tactful enough to keep his opinions to himself. But even though he may not always be willing to acknowledge the fact, he is always able to see the opposing point of view.

The symbolic beauty contest is taking place on the beach, and therefore an impromptu affair rather than a well-established event. This suggests that the subject is not particularly well organized himself. There is nothing to prevent him slipping away on his own, ignoring both the judges and the contestants. It seems he is unlikely to take himself too seriously, despite the sincerity of his feelings. Elements of both male and female are present within everybody. In this case the individual's "masculine" thoughts, representing the element of judgment, will be pertinent and openly available, though not necessarily freely expressed. His "feminine" feelings, representing submission to judgment, are likely to remain concealed. The deeper these feelings run, the more guardedly will they remain hidden.

The eastern or "soul-ego" degree will be 180°: *Dull routine is broken by an emergency call.* This seems to imply that the most personally pressing events in this soul-life are liable to occur suddenly. For long periods he may plod quietly along a routinely dull path; then, suddenly and apparently on a whim, routine will be shattered. Everything — career, social round, personal habits — will seem to change at once, and the whole course of his life may veer into entirely new directions. Once apprehended, his soul-life will seem to progress in a series of intuitive flashes rather than a gradually unfolding process of revelation. Because the Sun degree is split into opposing principles, these unpredictable surges of energy built into the driving force of the psyche may be all the more baffling. To his friends, Oliver is bound to appear temperamental; he will seem peacefully stable for months on end, but they know from experience that an eruption may occur at any time.

Next let us consider the western or descendant symbol of 360°. This occurs as a culmination of the span of reassurance, and completes the zodiac cycle: *A giant face has been carved into a mountain.* This symbol represents all the hopes of mankind; the creation of solid sculpture from mere plans, and real values from vague fantasies. But as a "giving out" point, as a *persona* of the soul, this solidity is not substantial in real life. Oliver may like people to believe that his achievements are wholly complete; this is the impression which he projects. But, counterbalanced by the other three points, the face and the mountain are both illusory. Oliver is not materialistically solid. Neither his achievements nor his shortcomings are of a tangible, historically solid type. The make-up of his soul ensures that, for him, creation is an ongoing and multi-directional process. His life's work will never be truly complete while he lives on this Earth, and despite any protestations to the contrary, he would have it no other way. The sum of his knowledge, and the sum of what he is prepared to tell, are not at all the same thing!

While the Sun degree registers a culmination of the span of striving, its polarity, the subjective degree of "soul-shadow", falls at the end of the span of freedom, 270°: *The pope is holding audience in the Vatican.* Every action or impulse that arises from this deep area of the soul, all his instinctive actions, good or bad, will have the flavour of religious approval. The conviction will be implicit that, once an impulse has arisen, like some *ex cathedra* doctrine of infallibility, it will be unimpeachably correct.

It is foregone that Oliver's sense of privacy will be strong, and his own feelings will certainly be kept well hidden. He will devise special methods of communication involving little routines that he expects others to respect. Like a real churchman, he may be alarmingly outspoken at times in condemning something that he feels to be wrong, but surprisingly broad-minded and forgiving over other occurrences that would shock the average person. He is certainly a person of conscience, but he will always remain aloof from the common herd. He gave permission for his birth chart to be analysed for this book, but I know he would prefer to remain a man of mystery.

All this, as a sketch of soul quality, has been surmised from the Sun sign alone. A horoscope cast in the traditional way, provided the time of birth is known, adds a purely personal element to the analysis. See chapter seven for David Oliver's chart. His birth took place during the first hour of ascending Scorpio — the span of memory, or recollection. According to this ascendant of the personality, he is a man who tends to live in the past; you might say that he broods. You will see that this tendency is modified by the subjective element now registered by the IC, the *imum coeli,* in the hour of anticipation. This is the source of the need to analyze and look for the deepest meanings. His personal unconscious mind will probably not be entirely unconscious, anticipating absorption into the collective unconscious itself. His objective southern point will be represented by the MC, or *medium coeli,* the true midheaven at the time of birth. This is in the hour of explanation; his aim will be set on interpretation, on searching, on finding out the whys and wherefores, and digesting that information.

Finally, on the descendant on the western extreme, we find that the cryptic element of submission corresponds with the hour of feeling. The implication is that his relationships, both with others whom he respects, and with the spiritual principle — with the Holy Spirit itself — will be of an emotional rather than an intellectual nature. Both collectively and personally, the "feeling" side of his character will be to the fore during all encounters and confrontations.

A point of decision

But let us return to the simple and seemingly non-specific — though in the inner sense actually more precise — collective chart based solely on the Sun's degree. As already mentioned, each hour or 15° span can be seen as a connecting stairway with three steps. At this point, perhaps, the distinction between inner and outer, between materiality and spirituality, will become clearer. Astrology applied to the inner self suggests that a psychological reversal of the standard evolutionary process is required if there is to be a meeting between mind and soul: to recover *dhyana,* the natural human instinct lost in babyhood, eventually perhaps to discover our own true law of living, our own *dharma.* It is the symbolic descent of this stairway, step by step, from the intellect through the emotions to regain and surmount the underlying instincts, that will actually prove to be an ascent to the source.

Natural evolution, shall we say, follows the sequence of the zodiac from 1° in Aires to 360° in Pisces. The first five degrees of the zodiac, stepping up or down, whichever way you choose to visualize it, represents the instinctive function, the second five degrees the emotional function, and the third five degrees the

147

intellectual function. This, we can assume, is the normal course of evolution from beast to human, from child to adult. To reverse the process, to climb back — again up or down in the imagination — entails quietening the mind and heart, symbolically tackling the first and second steps to reach the instinctual level of the first step. To become again like a little child is to reverse the evolutionary tendency towards strengthening materiality; to overrule the insistence of the intellect, and follow the emotional appeal of a search to recapture that original human instinct. The need for symbols will be left behind when the soul has finally regained that childlike state of receptivity. It will be open to receive the *dhyana* that motivates a newborn baby, the freely expressed movement of the wide-awake soul.

One's objective in life is normally a matter for the will, the application of heart and mind, non-instinctive and therefore forward-moving, evolutionary; but if that objective constitutes a *return* to the source, subordinating the conscious will through submission to the truly human instinctive function, then the sequence of that stairway, through the rest of that individual life, really will run backwards from the daily pursuit of worldly advancement, by way of the feelings, to regain those long-lost guiding instincts now intellectualized, perhaps as "intuition". As the universal becomes individual, so the individual becomes universal. In this case the individual' differentiation between "materiality" and "spirituality" is very evident.

If we follow three sets of five-degree steps forward from David Oliver's objective point of 90°, in the usual way according to the flow of evolution, we find symbols that seem to imply a wilful hardening and honing of the personality, leading towards a materialistic and, perhaps, an intemperate goal:

95° *A car driver races a train to the crossing;* a recklessly headlong dash through life pursuing questionable goals.

100° *A magnificent diamond is being cut to shape;* increasing sophistication, and an excessive appreciation of material values.

105° *Sated revellers rest after a banquet;* voracious self-seeking.

Interpretation cannot be made out of context, of course. If either a forward or a backward sequence is continued indefinitely, they will both arrive back at 90°; they are in reality the *same set* of symbols, the same individual staircase. But a reverse sequence, interpreted in the present context, seems to suggest a lighter, more "spiritual" nature, with an air of painless reformation:

85° *A gardener lovingly prunes his flowering shrubs;* one's train of thought and one's intention can be guided by discipline, without any hint of asceticism.

80° *A buffet luncheon with a lavish variety of food;* the inner feelings are freely available and richly varied.

75° *In a schoolroom, two children study together;* this suggests that the initial split is healed. A dual nature may represent outer and inner working together. Soul-life and personality are now in harmony, symbolizing the re-creation of a whole person.

At the peak of the human level, regained, there is no need for symbolism. But in the meantime the zodiac degree symbols offer an insight into the distinction between the qualities of ascending and descending. The "progressed point of self" traversing the zodiac should give significant results for most people, no matter which system has been used to ascertain it. Juggling with numbers can also give meaningful results, if the aim is known and sincerely expressed, for these results are intuitively gained.

Attempts have been made in the past to equate the wilful climb into occult realms with the apocalyptic number of the beast, 666. If we divide 360° by 666 we arrive at 0.54 (and 360 divided by 54 equals 6.66 recurring), and 54 can be taken as a constant, using sets of three degree symbols each separated by 54°. The degree on the point of self is taken to represent the present, with 54° on either side as a possible way forward. One could take the 84-year cycle, setting 1° at the birth date and multiplying the subject's age by a factor of 4.28 to find the progressed point of self (360 divided by 84 equals 4.28, or one years equals 4°16').

Let us take the case of Sarah Davis, born in the early morning of April 11, 1953 (Aries 21°). At the age of twenty-eight she told me that she felt she had reached a crossroads in her life. Within the threefold cycle she had certainly reached a crucial point, depending on her attitude of acceptance or rejection. 28 x 4.28 = 119.84 + 21 = 140.84 (141°). Suppose we set this degree on the nadir of the world mandala — the crucial point at which a decision has to be made: both ways are "up", so in which direction to climb?

141° has: *Farm animals become intoxicated on windfall apples.* This represents her current situation. 54° ahead at 195° has the symbol: *Precision-tooled wheels are stacked in a factory store.* And 54° back at 87° will have: *A gipsy child watches distant school children at play.*

At first sight, these three symbols may seem to have little in common, until we reflect on the nature of the life forces that form the zodiacal influence. The material influence is very clearly indicated under 195°, with precision-tooled wheels in a factory store. To symbolize Sarah's quandary there is a touch of natural comedy in the word-picture for 141°, with farm animals eating fermenting apples. The animal forces do not seem to be behaving in a typical manner; they seem adversely affected by the plant forces that should be beneath them.

Fermentation, of course, is a natural biological process that occurs when plant material is being broken down, and the micro-organisms responsible are quite possibly animal by nature. Drinking alcohol is a quick and effective way of imbibing the essence of plant forces and their associated passions! The symbol *could* indicate the end of the plant cycle — the decomposition of vegetation. The animals have the upper hand by helping the process along. On a personal scale, the animal influence with its robust desires *could* be in the process of replacing plant-arrogance as a personal centre of gravity.

Taken as a rising triad, the sequence seems to leave behind both material and vegetable influence, moving in essence to the animal realm. To say the a human is *rising* into the animal sphere of influence may seem ridiculous; we are all above the beasts. But we have already seen how the majority of people are centred low among the heavy forces of materiality. Few indeed are they who normally live even in the spiritual heights of the dumb animals!

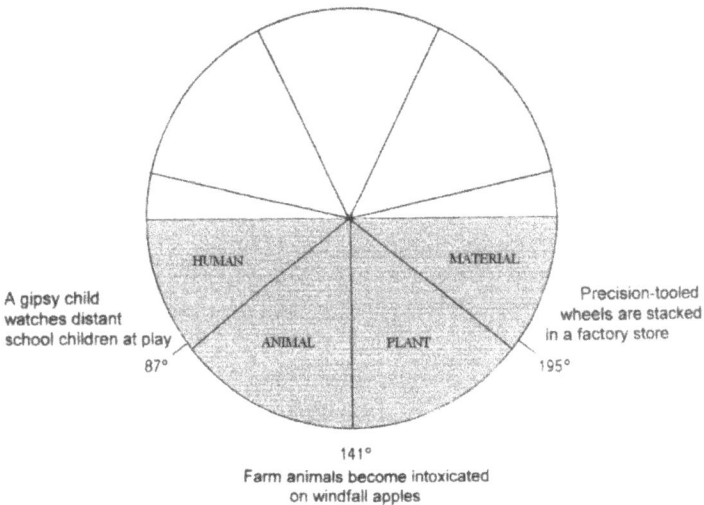

A gipsy child watches distant school children at play
87°

Precision-tooled wheels are stacked in a factory store
195°

141°
Farm animals become intoxicated on windfall apples

Crossroads : a Choice of Directions

For the possible future, or the *actual* past, under 87°, *A gipsy child watches distant school children at play,* the triad is completed with a most propitious omen: the subject seems destined to become human! It is interesting to extend the sequence on the diagram and discover that the equivalent of the ascendant (51°) has the spiritually submissive symbol: *A mysterious finger underlines passages in a book,* and the equivalent of the descendant at 231° is: *A young soldier goes absent to visit his wife* — truly a case of wilfully defiant passion!

To retrack the three symbols in the natural sequence of the zodiac, and the automatic direction inherited by mankind, is to follow the way of all flesh. In early childhood each individual was truly human, like the gipsy child wistfully watching the more "advanced" — that is, the more deeply entrenched in materiality and thus more privileged — older children.

Now, in the symbolic present, the notion of intoxicated animals may seem to carry a sinister overtone. The plant forces are again in charge, bringing the animals completely under their spell. The symbolic future now contains nothing but materiality — spiritually barren, perhaps, but full of culture, cleverness, skill and luxury.

So in this life there is no reversal of the course of evolution, of the great descent; not by willing it. It is time to look to the symbolic centrepoint of the birth chart — to that central point common to all. The strength of will can carry the seeker only as far as this: to find a contact with higher influences, with spirit; a contact that will initiate an unwilled inner climb back up the staircase of life.

CHAPTER 6

The planets as symbols

The planets are extraordinarily convenient symbols of synchronicity. They relate in regular measurable terms to their own central point of reference, the Sun, to their background, the zodiac, and equally they can be taken to relate to any place and any time on Earth — in our case, to the points of reference which make up the personal mandala of the birth chart. From this viewpoint the revolutions of these celestial bodies represent the sum of a constantly changing pattern of a larger environment, which may readily be compared with the ever-altering sequences of events upon the Earth and within ourselves. They are yet another readily observable and reliably predictable macrocosm relating to our microcosm, the impersonal many representing the personal one.

Taken alone, a symbol can have no meaning apart from itself, and the planets too can have no actual significance apart from their own material presence. When employed as symbols of life, however, they allow the cosmic existence of humankind to be studied as though it were the central feature of a coherent pattern. To the caveman, perhaps, these moving specks of light amongst fixed stars seemed full of life and meaning. And as intelligence developed, the ever-moving planetary system must have seemed a vast timekeeper with which they could measure human life and the earthly seasons, a reassuring hint of order surrounding, if not governing, a puzzlingly erratic world.

In synchronistic terms it was true in the Stone Age, and it is still true today: the many separate parts of cosmic interaction can be taken to represent the whole. Whatever the interests or motives of the seeker, the planetary pattern is something that can be identified as reliably precise, and consulted as a yardstick. But multiple whirling parts, as the wheels of a clock, can have time-keeping significance only when some kind of measuring device, as the hands of a clock, can be inserted, and the reading of that clock is seen to refer to a particular point in time, perhaps to record some special event. In astrology, this event is usually the point of birth as plotted on the birth chart. Measurements, however familiar, are fairly meaningless unless we have something that can be measured, and we understand the function of that "something". Astrology, too, can have no meaning without prior knowledge of the idea to be measured, the individual or the event which has come into being at that point in time and space.

The solar system is whole and complete in itself, and any such manifestation of wholeness outside of humanity can equally be used to symbolize our own inner state, to be understood as a kind of intuitive revelation. The unwilled and often unexpected phenomenon of highly significant symbols happens often in dreams, by way of the unconscious mind. The precept "seek and ye shall find" meets reality through the functioning of the collective soul, the pool of combined intuitive wisdom available to humankind. This really sums up the value of symbols as life-guides. Instinctive understanding readily becomes adulterated by individual passions, personal hopes and fears. Symbols are not the same as reality; they express reality only when that reality is not currently available, and there is no doubt that passionate misuse of symbols has led to innumerable superstitions and unpleasantnesses with which individuals and whole cultures and religions have encumbered themselves in the past, and often enthusiastically continue to do so.

Symbols work best for those who believe in them, who have faith that they will work. They can pilot the way to self-renewal, even to salvation, but they should be taken in moderation; the middle course is best. Half-hearted symbols are little more than a superstitious nuisance. At the other extreme, when taken as external reality, as supernatural forces of influence that compel, they can bring about all the woes that bigotry implies. At the risk of labouring the point, to believe that a symbol constitutes an external force is to court disintegration of the self. It is one of the symptoms of failure to evolve beyond the first cycle of houses — a clinging to ancestral beliefs. Extremes of fanaticism can arise when an abstract symbol is mistaken for material reality, as when people become convinced that their religion commands them to harm or kill others who seem to deny the symbol with which they have become identified.

Ripples in the pool of life

Astrologers take the Sun to represent the urge to wholeness in every sphere of life, not merely the spiritual aspirations of humanity. Having given life to the individual, and having, by means of the axial rotation of the Earth, presided over the very structure of our being, our horizons, the Sun comes to symbolize our own potential spiritual centre — a reflection of the potentiality of the Holy Spirit which brings all beings to the point of creative wholeness. As vitalizing power from the Sun distributes itself over the Earth, noonpoint is given special significance on the birth chart as the symbolic point at which all individuals may find their fullest, closest contact with that sustaining life force.

As recorded on the birth chart, the planets may be said to create points of activity on the equilibrium of that chart, or that life. They represent a disturbance in the pond, the ups and downs of fate. Those planets nearest to the Sun can be said to have significance for the human soul, but as they represent the outer qualities of thinking and feeling, during the quest for evidence of soul these inner planets must lose their symbolic power. Once the passions engendered by thoughts and emotions have been stilled, and a quiet sense of receptivity has been established in their stead, the symbolic significance of these fast-moving planets will vanish. Only then can the process of expansion begin.

Bounded by time in the guise of the Grim Reaper, Saturn, the innermost planets —Jupiter, Mars, Earth itself with its Moon, Venus and Mercury — can represent only those possibilities within us that are also bounded by time. We need to look outward towards the collective realm symbolized by Uranus, Neptune and Pluto. Jupiter can symbolize the pointer to show us the way. The ancient gods who shared their names with these planets represented the human functions, aspirations and limitations which the planets themselves now symbolize. The highest aspiration of a person ruled by Zeus, or Jupiter, was a place in the abode of gods — also controlled by Saturn, by the restriction of time. Greater possibilities by far lie beyond the bounds of time and through the symbolic sea of collective human feelings, to a greater destiny somewhere beyond the zodiac.

It is only when the functions expressed by the inner planets are actually stilled, when the heart and mind are allowed to subside in relaxation, that higher influences can be received. Such a non-feeling, non-thinking state sounds like sleep, or torpor, or hypnotic trance, or even death. But both Venus and Mercury are still in orbit — within and subservient to Earth's own bodily orbit around the Sun; they are now silent spectators. We do not want to lose their symbolic qualities, to lose consciousness; on the contrary! Our aim is the greatly enhanced awareness that voluntary freedom from these normal human functions can bring, whilst fully conscious and aware. The everyday functions of thinking and feeling should be subordinate to the truly conscious self, as the orbits of Mercury and Venus are contained within and thus subordinate to that of Earth.

This is why, in our astrology of the inner self, the fast-moving planets within the Earth's orbit may seem to be paid scant attention, the Moon still less. They must remain subservient to the whole Earth-being. Mercury, nimble messenger of the gods, is the symbol of thoughts — the highest function of evolution, that is, nearest the Sun; Venus, brilliant goddess of love, symbol of the emotional feelings, and the second highest function of evolution;

the Moon, wholly subordinate to Earth but essential to its well-being, influencing the flow of earthly and bodily fluids; all these represent progress on a *downward* spiral. They are part and parcel of the outer personality in symbolic terms, and if they can be ignored when preparing one's own birth chart, this omission may assist in charting the presence and progress of the inner self, and in assessing the receptivity of soul to spirit.

In traditional astrology, the inner planets whose orbits are embraced or surrounded by the orbit of the Earth itself, are said to refer to "conscious" and personal factors, the outer ones to "unconscious" and collective ones. We are adhering mainly to the latter because any study of the former will cover well-trodden ground, and we already know that territory well enough. The inner planets are normally used to symbolize the everyday personality, and within this term of reference their symbolism can work only on the individual level. They can have little significance for the collective life of humankind or, by that fact, for the life of the inner self.

Together with the Earth and the Moon, Venus and Mercury present a picture of the physical, emotional and mental being of the individual. The characteristics symbolized by Mercury, Venus, the Moon and even the Earth itself may now be seen as inferior to the truly human function; scarcely relevant, indeed, to human potentiality for spiritual expansion. When considering Mars, however, with its greater orbit, we can go beyond this strictly personal view of humankind. Mars "surrounds" the Earth symbolically with its aggressive male principle, its energy and its basic passions. Jupiter, greater still than Mars in size and orbit, in our cosmology can be taken to represent the human soul — the "ordinary lower soul" not to be mistaken for "spirit"; the soul which I have described as the receptacle of all influences, events, passions, thoughts, feelings and sensations. And Jupiter — the soul — is itself surrounded by the still greater orbit of Saturn.

Saturn, Kronos, Old Father Time, the Grim Reaper; death

itself, inevitably the rings around Saturn have been taken to symbolize the encircling limitations of time. Whereas space is unlimited, time is strictly limited. Time, in fact, is the universal limiting factor. And as the symbolic representative of time within our solar system, Saturn has traditionally been analogous with fate, the accumulation of karma.

Symbols of the collective unconscious

The outer planets Uranus, Neptune and Pluto, whose ancient traditions are in name only, being of comparatively recent discovery, symbolize for us the triad of the collective unconscious. Uranus, first of the three to be discovered, in astrological terms represents origination, the power of projection, and a channel for the unconscious mind to come to conscious awareness. Neptune, the next to be discovered, is said to record the assimilation, the storing, the breaking down and digesting, and the subsequent redistribution of that potent force. Pluto, the last to be discovered, represents for us the regenerative principle of that greater, that is, the collective, death and rebirth; a focus of collective power that normally remains on an unconscious level.

Uranus is enormous compared with Earth and, though so far away, is just visible at times to the naked eye. In our language of symbolism, these periods of drawing closer to Earth may be synchronized with times when images from the collective unconscious can most readily reach our awareness. The Uranus revolution around the Sun takes eighty-four years, and in this equates to the Lifespan of the Patriarch — the life of collective humanity — a completion of the threefold cycle.

In its traditional interpretation, Uranus is said to express great nervous energy, heralding the arrival of what may be a creative genius or a violent crank. It always suggests an urge to be inwardly different, to climb out of the rut of conventionality and orthodoxy. In other words, Uranus may be a symbol of the eccentric. But Uranus should more correctly be seen as a collective symbol, and there is more than one type of "individuality". A person may remain outwardly conventional within his or her society, whilst inwardly becoming utterly different; transformed. True spirituality, be assured, has no need of fancy dress, and seldom appears in unconventional garb.

To astrologers of the inner self, Uranus represents Mars on a collective scale. Where Mars symbolizes the passions which surround the individual, Uranus symbolizes the "collective passions". In this sense, Uranus is the measure of symbols of the unconscious mind as they are sometimes brought to awareness through dreams. It represents the source both of the inspiration and of the vague idea — the "answer from the inner self" that comes when one is hard pressed, and when other possibilities have been surrendered. Such images are the seeds of new ideas, and may be of the greatest breakthrough value for the scientist, or the inspired crusade for social reformers. Poets and artists also frequently have a favourable aspect with Uranus in their chart.

Neptune takes almost one hundred and sixty-five years to complete its orbit. As a symbol, this planet implies an extraordinary sensitivity to whatever lies deeply hidden within oneself — the seat of wholeness. Its synchronistic possibilities show themselves when great creative talents appear, and its aspects feature strongly at the birth of a sage or mystic, and later, when they come into contact with collective forces, with their spiritual awakening.

Because of this potency of its synchronistic qualities, Neptune seems sometimes to impel the subject of a birth chart to follow whatever lies within his inner feelings, and when this cannot happen for whatever reason, it will signal bouts of depression, or other strange and unpleasant reactions. For this reason it has often been thought by astrologers actually to cause odd behavioural traits; but strange behaviour symbolized by Neptune is rather like medicinal purging — it may be extremely unpleasant, both to those nearby and to the subject personally, but it has the effect of cleansing and purifying the inner self.

Neptune then seems to point the way to higher things, and appears to aspect most strongly in cases where spiritual love and compassion are able to fruit. It always represents a broadening of horizons. As a symbol of the collective soul it represents that greater than individual factor which prevents the earthly ego becoming too powerful or self-satisfied, which avoids narrow mindedness and over-pious limitations of perception.

Yes, Neptune is certainly a potent symbol of inner growth, of the soul that has become filled with divine inspiration. As a symbol too of the sea, it represents that great tide of inner feeling that is to be overcome by the spiritual seeker: the ocean to be swallowed or swum; the towering tidal wave in which to be washed unharmed. Neptune represents the force — the strength of the inner feelings — that lures the ordinary person into spiritual adventure; into seeking the highest of goals. To us, it has to represent Jupiter on a collective scale — the collective soul of humankind.

Because Pluto is so small and so far away, and because its orbit of the Sun is so erratic, sometimes cuttings across the path of Neptune, it may as well be called a comet as a planet, despite having its own satellite — Charon. Scientists voted in 2006 as to how they should define Pluto, and decided that it should be relegated to the status of 'minor planet'. From our point of view Pluto will loiter for thirty-odd years in passing through some signs of the zodiac, and speed through others in little more than a dozen. It will take some two hundred and forty-eight years to complete a full orbit of the Sun, and at the time of writing we have seen less than a third of that orbit since its discovery in 1930. The year 1989 saw it passing relatively close to the Sun before again wending its laborious way through the outer reaches of the solar system.

There have been numerous suggestions as to the significance of Pluto as a symbol. It is said by most astrologers to represent the actual process of elimination or purification within the subconscious mind. It hints at the consequent revelation of previously hidden contents; it implies a change of attitude or function; and it has been said to symbolize a trigger-point for fanatical extremism, ethnic cleansing, gangsterism and mob rule.

But though of so collective a nature, the symbol of Pluto needs to be understood on a personal basis. Any stirring or partial opening of the normally sealed depths of the unconscious mind, on a public or "tribal" scale, can produce these dark outpourings. But the same change of perception that can provoke a mob to violence may prove a far more desirable feature in the individual, setting in motion a cleansing of the soul. There is no doubt in my mind that Pluto can symbolize the type of coming together that may result in spiritual rebirth. It is not the symbol of the lone fakir or the self-contained yogi. It refers to a coaxing open of the encrusted soul, to the loss of coarse impulses, and the receiving of finer and less selfish influences. It can well symbolize the collective process of inward growth for a group of like-minded souls.

Orbiting where the Earth's own influence represented by the zodiac is scarcely operative, nearest to what we might think of as the great unknown beyond our solar system, Pluto represents the cosmic transmitter — the mysterious stepping-off point. We can now say that it represents Saturn, but on a collective scale — lord, not of time, but of the zodiac itself, bounden only by space. Its aspects can plot the opening and entry into the inner self, its discovery and the mind's reaction to it. Having been awakened by Uranian dreams, baptized in the Neptunian sea, the collective rebirth is signalled by Pluto: the becoming again like a little child.

For many centuries before the discovery of the outer planets, the human view of our cosmos was exclusively geocentric. With their evolving, downwards-developing souls, our ancestors were orientated towards the distant possibilities of material progress. By following the natural sequence of passions, they would feel d rawn towards a destiny that seemed higher than that symbolized by the encircling Sun and Moon. These two attendant deities they would have seen as intimately concerned with the physical needs of nature and everyday life, playing the roles of hero and heroine in their daily and nightly routines and essential for earthly well-being, but not responsible for human destiny. The planetary gods of fate would have been seen as conducting their affairs in the space above and between these reassuringly familiar presences. Religious aspirations would have been slanted towards the cycle of time, and thus towards the distant ruler of all cycles — Saturn. The festival of the saturnalia, with all that it entailed, and with all its numerous worldwide variations, was always the most popular, the most obvious, the most directly inspired, the most instinctively motivated celebration in people's lives. Saturn seen as a living principle, was god-overseer and father of Zeus or Jupiter. Jupiter in his turn was god-judge of all souls, and undisputed king of all heavens within the boundaries of time.

To take the later, heliocentric view, the Sun draws the process of evolution down towards itself through its life-giving energy. Closest to the Sun, the god-messenger Mercury represents the mind and its powers of thought. The evening star Venus symbolizes the feelings — the emotions. The Moon symbolizes and, indeed, actually influences the bodily functions and the apparatus of sensation. But all these are bounded now by the passions, by the male principle of Mars pointing away from the Sun, away from the Earth, towards unknown realms beyond the time-bound limits of Saturn.

But Mars could equally well symbolize the channel by which we humans are made able to receive impulses higher than those belonging to the normal, everyday senses. All the planets with orbits greater than that of Earth could well be thought of as receptacles for those impulses. Astrology in relation to the inner self pays scant attention to the inner planets, not because their symbolism is false, or because we wish to appear superior, but because they represent only those factors that refer to the physical individual. Thoughts and feelings are essential for us all; we are

THE PLANETS AS SYMBOLS

simply looking for higher possibilities.

We have seen how the driving passions, symbolized by Mars, surround the physical vessel of Earth by its orbit. But the human soul, albeit the "lower soul" symbolized by Jupiter, encompasses these passions within its own orbit. The soul, Jupiter, the original Zeus, is indeed the halfway house, able to receive and contain simultaneously the base passions, feelings, thoughts, and such finer influences as may filter in from beyond Saturn, the symbol of mortality.

Saturn's orbit defines the limit of individuality. Death confines the personal human soul and its contents, as well as the body and the mind. But we know by experience that there is a channel through which outer influences may flow inwards. We have moved beyond mere symbolism now. When we speak of fate and the varied traits of human affairs, the planets certainly symbolize "influences" . But having acknowledged this, we are not thereby denying the existence of more subtle, more real, more divine influences from beyond.

BOUND BY SPACE
    Pluto
    Neptune
    Uranus

BOUND BY TIME
    Saturn
    Jupiter
    Mars

BOUND BY MATERIALITY
    Earth
    Moon
    Venus
    Mercury

INTEGRATING PRINCIPLE
    Sun

Having achieved contact with the channel of non-personal influences, the passions of Mars can "become" the collective passions of Uranus. Uranus will then no longer seem the symbol of cranks and eccentric seers, as it does to many conventional astrologers, because it is indeed the "seat of images from the collective unconscious". Those strange and fantastic perceptions which have long been sensed as "mysterious" will at last take on wholly reasonable shape.

The personal soul of Jupiter can "become" the collective soul of Neptune and, by receiving the flow of collective contents, the heavier, lower base passions will be forced out of their hiding place. There are many people alive today who have experienced this, though they may have no use for symbols, and they may not speak of planets. Nevertheless in this symbol — the collective soul of Neptune — all people are linked.

This is the truth of it: the inner self includes and combines the personal and the collective selves. The physical body will still be bound by grim-faced Saturn, the symbol of death. But remember that the innermost planets symbolize what we perceive as physical realities: Mercury, Venus, Earth, Moon, and to a lesser extent, Mars, all these are the solidly rock-based symbols of our physical being. Beyond Mars the visible planets, largely gaseous, must symbolize the non-physical, intangible aspects of humanity. Death, to the soul which has found its own higher purpose, will simply be death to the extent of Mars — the extinction of Earth-bound passions. The timekeeper Saturn's power over destiny will have been broken; Saturn in the inner perception will have "become" Pluto, symbolic keeper of the frontier to a greater world beyond the zodiac. In this role Pluto will be sure to feature strongly in the birth chart of one who has made contact with a life force greater than that usually known by earthly minds.

The blueprint of life

What does it mean, exactly, to say that a planet "features strongly"

164

in a birth chart, or indeed that it "features" at all? Firstly, the very fact that it appears on the chart, within a certain degree of the zodiac, implies that it does indeed "feature", and can be used as a meaningful symbol. It features more strongly when the time of birth is known well enough to allow us to plot the mundane house, the psychological compartment of the self, in which the planet appears. It features more strongly still when by its position it forms a recognized aspect, or angular relationship, with other planets, with the ascendant, or with other significant points in the chart.

We already have a firm idea of the distinctive brand of cosmic energy traditionally associated with each planet, the type of psychic impulse which it symbolizes. We can refer also to the instinctive quality — the dreamlike quality understood by the inner feelings — ascribed to each degree of the zodiac in which a planet may make its appearance. We can see how the quality of a particular degree accentuates and colours and focuses the stream of cosmic energy symbolized by that planet; and we can apply those qualities, modified and blended, to the appropriate mundane house — to the area of psychological concern within which they will chiefly operate.

Even a "weakly" featuring planet will have formed at least one significant aspect in the birth chart, by virtue of its conjunction with the degree in which it appears. We can now see that it will accentuate the characteristics of that degree, the significance of the degree symbol, in its own unique way. Degree quality and planetary energy: a series of such points of emphasis can bring out the essential qualities of an individual in an imaginative way, a way that will stir and develop a refreshing capacity for intuitive appreciation.

If the time of birth is known accurately enough to permit the mundane houses to be plotted, remember to note the position of a planet with regard, not only to the house itself as an area of awareness or phase of the soul, but also in relation to its position within the house. Appearing close to the entry cusp of a house, the planet can be taken to signify a new awareness of the quality that is being symbolized. If it appears towards the end of a house, it will represent rather a fulfilment of the quality it expresses. The ascendant itself indicates the quality of uniqueness; and the relationship of the ascendant to the Sun and the planets symbolizes the type of psychic activity that best characterizes the individual who is seeking a closer liaison with, and a more intimate knowledge of, the greater self.

It is advisable, I think, to forget the old idea of interpreting planetary aspects as though they were fixed "influences". We need to consider them as synchronistic indicators of what is already there within the self, waiting to be uncovered. We need to read the personal mandala of the birth chart as the blueprint of a life, a plan of all its possibilities. The start of a new life is merely a phase in a progressive event, and not a once-for-all occurrence. By analyzing the blueprint, by pondering on the sequence of degree symbols, and by plotting the transits of the outer planets, the interpreter should be able to "see" the course of that life unfolding. The birth chart is like an architect's plan of a projected building. The better the builder understands his trade, the clearer will he be able to assess when each phase is due to be completed, and what the building should look like on completion.

It is useful to reconsider the concept of horizon and meridian on the birth chart in relation to the position of the planets at birth. It is desirable too not to forget the psychological functions symbolized as occupying the four quarters of the chart. In general terms, when all the planets are sited above the horizon, the subject is likely to seem most strongly affected by external, objective events. Conversely, when the planets are concentrated below the horizon, the subject is likely to have a subjective outlook on life. He or she will tend to be introverted, and emotionally rather than intellectually inclined. Such a person will seem, perhaps, less interested in facts than in ideas, inclined to follow the promptings of intuition rather than logic.

A bias of planetary grouping according to the sequence of the zodiac is often found to have significance too: when all slow-moving planets are placed within the first half of the zodiac, between Aries and Libra, the emphasis of the individual life will tend to be "spiritual"; where they are grouped in the latter half, between Libra and Aries, the subject's preoccupations will seem to be materially orientated. The odd one out — a planet that stands alone in one section of the chart opposing the majority — may serve to emphasize rather than detract from these points.

Planetary aspects

The interplay of planetary aspects fits into the blueprint of an unfolding life by indicating tendencies towards a particular end. It is misleading to consider them ends in themselves. In effect, any aspect is, potentially, part of a symmetrical polygon, and when that polygon shows itself as completed, perhaps through the subsequent transits of the planets, the symbol will be complete. We can expect the tendency it portrays to reach fulfilment during the period indicated.

Traditional astrology sometimes tends to polarize the implications of planetary aspects as either good or bad, and frequently they are thought of as influences, or impacts on a life, rather than indications or tendencies. But when using astrology to help gain some inkling of the inner self, it is best to forget about good or bad, fortunate or unfortunate. Ideas of this sort are best limited to the outer personality, to matters of the will; our system explores conditions that are not really subject to ethical choice.

From this point of view, aspects based on the triangle, or trine, traditionally reckoned favourable and fortunate, represent periods of creative possibility, hinting at a new way of thinking, a new direction in life, a new understanding. Aspects based on the square, traditionally thought of as obstructive and unfortunate, to us indicate the actuality of these new beginnings; they represent the circumstance that may allow those creative impulses towards renewal to be put into practice, and they suggest the trigger which can change the course of a life.

The aspects between square and trine represent all those factors in between, all the significances that may occur between the first realization that spiritual attainment is needed, and the impulse to actually set the wheels in motion, the spiritual journey that will culminate in real fulfilment. They represent the subtleties, the stages of psychic realization, the potential of creative capacity, the nature and quality of individual contents.

A conjunction which involves the outer, "collective" planets, and in particular when Saturn too is involved, carries the implication of a usually violent release of activity. Saturn can be taken to represent the "break-through point" between inner and outer, between the individual and the collective life, and a great deal of energy, in psychic terms, is massed at this point. An aspect can have no spiritual significance in itself, but conjunctions such as this always constitute a psychological crossroads, a choice to be made between positive or negative uses of inner energy.

When two planets are in opposition, they sometimes seem to be calling for a reconciliation of opposite points of view. An attraction of polarities may be the inference in positive life situations, but where opposites seem to clash, the outcome can be destructively negative. In one direction may lie an expansion of consciousness, in the other, psychological confusion. A powerful opposition can signify a time of outward disintegration, but it may also involve the subordination of the outer personality to inner values. Where an opposition involves the ascendant or the descendant, the MC, the zenith or the nadir, the aspect should be understood in terms of potential consciousness of factors that were previously unconscious, a coming to vivid awareness.

An aspect of opposition can be seen as having a positive and a negative pole — though not necessarily with wholly undesirable long-term results. It may imply neutralization of what might have been destructively opposing factors. Stressful results are more nearly to be predicted in cases of near, or inexact opposition. Near opposition implies that intense psychic activity is taking place between two extremes, and the outcome can be expected to be more dramatic than in the case of exact opposition.

Most commonly used aspects

Conjunction (0°)	signifying basic activity, powerful emphasis on whatever the planets represent, and a stimulation of their functions.
Opposition (180°)	signifying awareness and interaction between functions, but with possible tension or inner conflict.
Trine (120°)	signifying harmony, being at peace with oneself, the resolution of conflict and the principle of creation.
Square (90°)	signifying construction through necessity, powerful release of feelings involving outward determination, often accompanied by inward conflict.
Sextile (60°)	signifying production or creative activity brought about through submission to a higher (perhaps divine) authority; an abnegation of personal will.

Less commonly used aspects

Quintile (72°)	signifying the nature of the innermost passions, the inner level of being, or soul quality.
Septile (51°26')	signifying death of the will, or release of the passions that hold the soul captive.
Semi-square (45°) *Sesquiquadrate* (135°) *Hendecagon* (32°43')	signifying some special awareness of inner factors, depending on inheritance, karma, and the indications of the birth chart as a whole.
Nonagon (40°) *Semi-sextile* (30°) *Quincunx* (150°)	signifying new stages of creative impulses not involving the coarse outer will, and of importance to the developing self.
Semi-quintile (36°) *Bi-quintile* (144°)	signifying the potential union of soul qualities, and their assimilation by the inner self.

The aspects most commonly used in astrology relate chiefly to the outer personality, but they can provide valuable insights in our present context too, in terms of realization, and impulse. The tolerance or so-called "orb of influence" for these aspects — their approximation — extends to a diminishing extent for a few degrees (perhaps up to 7°) on either side of the actual angular degree. Less commonly used aspects with more subtle implications should not be allowed any tolerance. These are usually best applied in respect of the slow-moving outer planets, Uranus, Neptune and Pluto.

Running backwards

Depending on the appearance of its orbit as seen from Earth, a planet will sometimes appear to be backtracking on itself. On the birth chart the plotting of a planet's course as "direct" or "retrograde", or indeed if it appears to be stationary at the time of birth, can hint at different qualities of awareness. When a planet, from our viewpoint, seems to be moving particularly fast, its "flow of energy" is said to be equally quick-acting and short-lasting; when, at the other extreme, a planet appears to be very slow or stationary, the function which is symbolizes will seem equally stubborn and fixed in the individual psyche.

A strongly placed stationary planet, when sited in the "unconscious" area of the chart, below the horizon, will always register a peculiarly stubborn, in some ways obtuse attitude in that field. Retrograde planets signify a "regression" of the energy they represent, a turning back from the conscious to the unconscious layers of mind; a certain defensiveness, perhaps, in that particular area of expression. A retrograde planet, or the type of energy it represents, seems somehow to have bypassed the normal mode of expression, becoming focused instead on the under-belly of the mind, working subconsciously from below.

Uranus can be said to plot the course of inner purification

after the process has already begun, rather than its initiation. Retrograde, it can symbolize some kind of blockage or barrier to smooth progress. There will certainly be such psychic upheavals as are necessary (and they frequently are) to allow ongoing purification of the inner feelings to advance. There seem to be no secrets of the soul when Uranus is running retrograde. Deeply collective as well as purely personal soul-contents tend to be projected outwards, and the images and new understandings that are produced can be of benefit to others. It is as if the collective soul itself can become to a certain extent demystified by their projection. At such times, instead of these images remaining hidden and unsuspected, they become available to all who may seek them.

Neptune often seems to highlight the religious sensibilities of the individual. People in whose chart Neptune is retrograde can usually see straight to the heart of religious matters. There is no pulling the wool over their eyes, and they are not impressed by piety or ritual. The only thing that seems to matter to them is reality, first of the personal soul, then of the collective soul, and thereby the ultimate reality. A direct Neptune "allows" people to be conventionally religious; Neptune running retrograde "forbids" it.

Saturn is said by most astrologers to be the ego-builder, and in those cases where Saturn is retrograde at birth it seems that the ego cannot be developed in the normal way to act as a defence mechanism against the slings and arrows of life. Instead of being fortified against the outside world, such people may appear oddly vulnerable, not necessarily shy, but introverted to a marked extent. Their strength of selfhood will be proportionately turned inwards; their "ego" will function not in their outer but in their inner feelings. Their confidence, their invincibility, will reside in the soul and not in the personality. Retrograde Saturn is a feature usually to be found in the charts of those who live their lives, to some extent, on the inner plane.

Various methods are used by astrologers to assess planetary

"influence" — or to predict the events represented by their movements and aspects — at any given period of the birth chart native's life. Progression, a completely symbolic technique for projecting planetary movements forward in time, usually substituting a "year for a day", can really apply only to the fast-moving inner planets, and thence to the outer self. Plotting the transits of the slower-moving planets, however, is always useful. It involves superimposing on the birth chart the actual planetary positions for any later date, using an ephemeris for the year in question. This method can prove a valuable aid when studying the blueprint of life, when looking for future possibilities and past explanations.

CHAPTER 7

Exploring personal trends

Casting a horoscope, calculating a birth chart, is a way of using symbols to ask questions and receive answers about the quality and potentiality of the moment. Predictions have a habit of proving often to be wrong; I dare say they are usually wrong. When astrological predictions prove equally wrong this does not prove that astrology is wrong or meaningless, any more than a mistaken mathematical theory will prove that mathematical calculations are useless. Symbols can have no real meaning of their own; they are useful only to the extent that the subject to which they are applied is well understood. With this proviso, they can serve to identify and determine facts and substantiate theories, to stabilize wildly variable possibilities.

Astrology of the inner self has to *begin* with an intuitive understanding of the soul, to be substantiated sooner or later by practical experience. As the inner self in its broadest sense embraces the whole collective self of humankind, it already includes all systems of understanding within itself. To regard our type of astrology as an amalgam of this and that system, to analyze bits of it, is to misunderstand its nature and purpose. Certainly our system has to contain elements of natal astrology which, as it depends for objective accuracy on assumed knowledge of the exact moment of birth, is largely subjective. It will contain elements of mundane astrology, "astrology of the Earth", because this deals largely with collective moods and broad-scale psychological changes. The Earth is the seat and the symbol of the individual self, and it has inescapable associations with each zodiac degree, which again are of great importance for the individual.

The inner self, as the seat of the soul, contains elements of past, present and future on an individual and a collective scale. Looking at world-scale events, collective moods often seem chaotic. This is by no means a modern phenomenon; the same applies now as in ancient times. What may be chaotic collectively can prove an inspirational new beginning personally, and when individual passions are stilled, the collective mood too will be quiet and receptive. It is when the individual is in a state of quiet receptivity that mundane astrology holds the most significance. Many astrologers are unaware of the possibility of observing, sensing and receiving divine influences in stillness. It is at the point of *uncalculated* stillness — that is, during the absence of desire — that *real* influence may be felt.

I aim to draw attention to the possibilities of quiet submission to such fine influences as may underflow or transcend the "personality" of daily experience. Personality, it is true, could be said to constitute the whole person as he or she functions in the world. I do not want to imply that "personality" refers only to the "outer" and thus not to the inner self. Without personality, I suppose, there could be no person in any meaningful sense.

But by over-valuing "mind", the intellectual viewpoint tends to see "personality" as a potential expression of wholeness in itself. As Dane Rudhyar wrote: *The goal of astrology is the alchemy of personality. It is to transform chaos into cosmos, collective human nature into individual and creative personality.* It is mainly a matter of definition. I am taking "personality" to mean a synthesis of patterns of behaviour brought about through the will, and the main purpose of this book is to formulate the possibility of inner growth towards wholeness, which can take place only when the will itself, and thereby the personality too, has been temporarily suspended. The soul, like that of a newborn child, would have no personality in this sense, if it did not become superimposed in the form of influences from without. It is the self without this imposition that we need to consider, and this ought not to be taken as a theory, but as potential experience.

174

With this definition of personality in mind, there is a point to be made about the mundane houses taken as representatives of the soul. They should be seen as equal in size and capacity in every case. The soul lives and may come to its own awareness in time, but its substance is not of "time", but of "space". It is best then, when astrologically pursuing an interest in the inner self, to make use of the Equal House System when plotting the houses, rather than the Placidean System which is based on the Earth's rotation. Thirty years after the publication of *Astrology of Personality* Rudhyar wrote: *...now I conceive the houses most definitely as 30-degree sections of space surrounding the natal act of individualization, i.e., the first breath which establishes the individual rhythms of the newborn. The houses are not in the zodiac; but it is the signs of the zodiac and all the celestial bodies which find their location in this or that house. As a result, the Placidus system of house-determination, which is still mostly in use, does not fit in with such an approach, for it is based on a time-factor.* Soul "personality" cannot vary according to the latitude in which the individual is born. The Placidean System results in gross distortion of the houses on the birth chart of anyone born, say, in Norway or Alaska, and to quote the British astrologer Jeff Mayo: *If a system cannot be applied to the whole sphere of the Earth, wherever birth occurs, it is worthless.* Everyone has to start off with the same psychic field of potential action, the same expanse of virgin soil in which their garden can grow. The personal charts given in this book make use of the Equal House System for these reasons.

Dane Rudhyar was intellectually creative, a fact hinted at by his birth chart ascendant degree (rectified by himself) standing as it does in quintile aspect with Mercury — his thoughts were able to express the passions of his soul — and amply demonstrated by his expertise and taste in music. Whilst studying at the Paris Conservatoire he had become an admirer of Claude Debussy, and his book on that musician's life was published when he still only eighteen years of age. Debussy's so-called "allusive vagueness" appealed to him as poetic ideas translated into musical tone.

Debussy at that time was at the forefront of the "Impressionist" school of music, doing with tone more or less what the Impressionist painters were doing with light. Rudhyar was fascinated too by the pioneer work of the Russian composer Alexander Scriabin, who related his music to what he felt were its spiritual roots, and to whom light and tone were indeed interwoven. Scriabin's *Prometheus,* or "Poem of Fire", actually included a score-line for *tastiera per luce,* a "keyboard of light" which produced an accompanying display of coloured lights projected onto a screen.

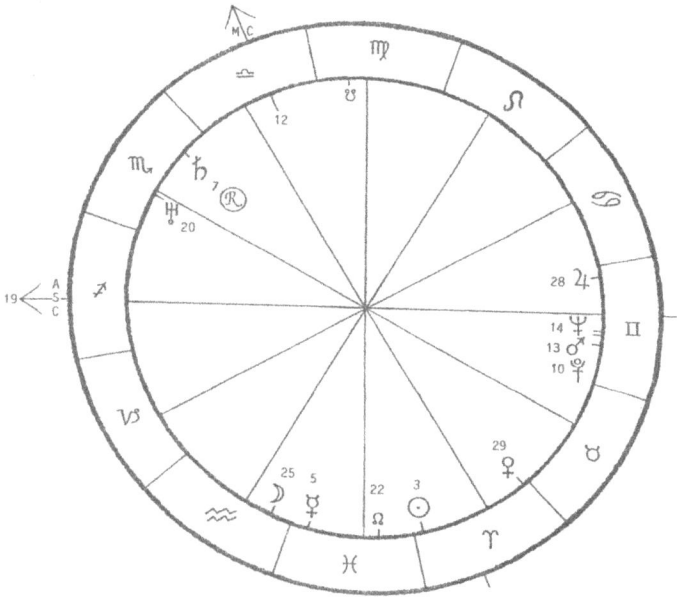

Birthchart of Dane Rudhyar

On his birth chart Venus sextile with Jupiter whilst in opposition to Saturn illustrates his appreciation of beauty and unusual harmony, and the interaction between two extremes — the aesthetic and the logical — which seems to lie at the root of his

176

compositions. The Mars-Neptune-Pluto conjunction in his sixth house, forming a quintile aspect with his Sun and a trine with his MC, seems to strengthen this principle of harmonic polarity.

Rudhyar based his early musical compositions on Scriabin's pioneering work, and *Prometheus* inspired his own tone-poem, *Surge of Fire,* or "Soul Fire", which won him the Los Angeles Orchestra Music Award a few years later. His complex rhythms and swelling chords produced a recondite type of music which has baffled many traditional music lovers, and defied most musicologists' attempts to classify it, their descriptions ranging from "intellectually absolute" to what might be thought its antithesis: "mystical program music".

Rudhyar — or Daniel Chenneviére as he was then known —left Paris and emigrated to Canada in 1914, settling in French-speaking Quebec, his move coinciding with the outbreak of World War 1. The disruption was signalled on the chart, perhaps, by his natal Sun squaring with the transitted "World War conjunction" of Pluto with Saturn within 3° Cancer (symbol: *An arctic explorer drives his dog team*), as less-than-human forces seemed to draw humanity rapidly into an unknown and coldly merciless future. Mercury, by its squaring with Mars and Pluto and its trine with Saturn, implies an inbuilt awareness of an impending life-cycle best avoided, and the personal determination to do just that. In this respect he resembled other philosophically-minded intellectuals of his time, notably George Gurdjieff and Peter Ouspensky, who also moved far enough afield to avoid involvement in the mindless struggle which they foresaw.

Finding Quebec culturally and socially disappointing, Chenneviére moved to the USA in 1916 and lived in New York. There, finding that New Yorkers did not care to attempt to pronounce his name correctly, at the age of twenty-one he changed it to the imaginative Dane Rudhyar, by which he was to become well known. His choice of name was inspired by the Sanskrit *rudh-irá,* with the sense of "Red Planet". He had probably felt himself to be identified in some way with the planet Mars when he first took an interest in astrology. The position of Mars on his chart, giving the symbolic word-picture: *A virtuoso pianist begins his concert,* seemed particularly apt, as expressive of his ambitions and interests. The choice of name reflects too his fascination with Hindu philosophy which he had studied at the Sorbonne. Interpreted in his own way, through harmony, through music, that interest resulted in his book *The Rebirth of Hindu Music* which was published in 1929 (though it had been conceived many years earlier), said to have been a somewhat visionary and theosophical distillation of Hinduism and its distinctive musical styles.

He left New York in 1919 and moved again, this time to Southern California. There he enjoyed a brief dalliance with Hollywood, and actually played a major role in a silent film — the part of Jesus in Cecil B De Mille's epic, *The Ten Commandments.* Plainly he was thought to look the part, and his natal Sun square with Jupiter seems to testify that he was not without the necessary touch of conceit which would enable him to carry it off.

Though he had inherited all the Gallic charm expressed by Mercury sextile with Venus, he could, from all accounts, be a somewhat difficult person to live with. His Moon square with Uranus suggests that he could be argumentative, and his Mars square with Mercury also bears witness to the occasional irritable outburst. During his life he was married four times. Scepticism of the type associated with a Sorbonne education can be exasperating when one is on the receiving end; but Rudhyar's approach to astrology, once he had become acclimatized to the USA (he became an American citizen in 1926) was refreshingly worthwhile, penetrating to the heart of his subject, rejecting the pseudo-scientific approach and the "event orientated", divinatory features which he considered plagued it. He brought out its true value as a holistic art dedicated to the potential blossoming of the inner self.

His Sun quintile with Neptune in its near conjunction with Mars and Pluto seems to confirm his penetrating approach to astrology. His creative, artistic tendencies and deep-rooted mysticism expressed themselves effortlessly, assertively, almost obsessively. His Mercury trine with Saturn and Jupiter symbolized his ability to think deeply about soul matters in philosophical terms. Most of all, perhaps, his chart expresses the driving need which he felt, to bring his personal message to the collective awareness; to penetrate the unquestioning assumptions of his day; to bring out all the basic truths about life which he knew to be hidden and waiting discovery.

In the fullness of time

The birth chart, as I am sure all astrologers will agree, should be considered as a whole; the gathering of all factors to the individual case. Wholeness is, after all, our ultimate aim. But it is easier said than done; the kind of wholeness requiring minutiae of detail tends to embrace the outer personality exclusively, and we need to look beyond, as well as within, our own orbit. Even clever minds tend towards a somewhat negative understanding of time, and the creative wholeness latent within each moment is readily overlooked. The keen mind works to analyze its perceptions, and analysis, by definition, breaks the subject down into understandable parts; quite unwittingly therefore it tends to deprive potential wholes of their possibility of wholeness. But without thought, of course, we will get nowhere, and some sort of analysis is necessary, if only to supervise the intuitive process of perceiving the whole.

When using astrology as a tool with which to study the inner self, one can skip fairly lightly over the purely physical factors, the bodily sensations and moods as symbolized by the Moon, and even the functions of thinking and feeling, the mind and the heart, as symbolized by Mercury and Venus; these also are products of the material body. The positions of Sun and outer planets, on the other hand, should be accurately noted with their zodiac degree. If the time of birth is known, we will also have the house positions and thereby the ascendant degree. When the time of birth is unknown, by tradition the chart is set for noon. For experimental purposes, as a picture of personal progress, the chart may even be set with the ascendant at the cusp of Aries, at the spring equinox, because this is the symbolic point of rebirth for the Earth in its symbolic guise as an individual.

The birth chart ascendant, according to its traditional interpretation, indicates the manner in which a person finds individuality. The horizon, or horizontal axis, divides the world between seen and unseen, conscious and unconscious. The zenith meridian separates those things connected with the individual will, one's own volition, on the eastern rising side, from those things on the western descending side which do not come about from the will.

Thoughts, therefore, can be said to linger in the east, whilst feelings tend to congregate in the west. This is straight forward enough in traditional astrological interpretations where thinking and feeling are probably the chief means by which the individual personality is described and recognized. The principle is also significant when considering the inner self, but not quite in the same way. It is not the functions of thought and feeling themselves that are being analyzed in this case; but they are the vehicles by which the everyday outer mind approaches matters of soul and spirit in order to understand them. For instance, when Mars, Saturn and Neptune are to the east (as they are in David Oliver's birth chart), then the drive to take part in some kind of spiritual awakening, the method, the timing, and the duration involved, as well as one's attitude towards established religion, will tend to be regulated by the thinking mind. With Jupiter and Uranus in the western zone however, deeper experiences in this field, the functioning of the soul itself, and the process of integrating higher influences, will be very much a matter for the feelings.

In this example, all the slow-moving planets, with the exception of Saturn, appear within the first half of the zodiac, between Aries and Virgo, emphasizing the "spiritual" side of the chart native's life. The isolated position of Saturn within that quarter of the chart associated with intuition confirms this bias. Its symbolic role is to act as an intuitive trigger. Its degree symbol: *A defeated general hands over his sword with dignity,* seems to imply potential sacrifice of material benefits for purely abstract, inner values.

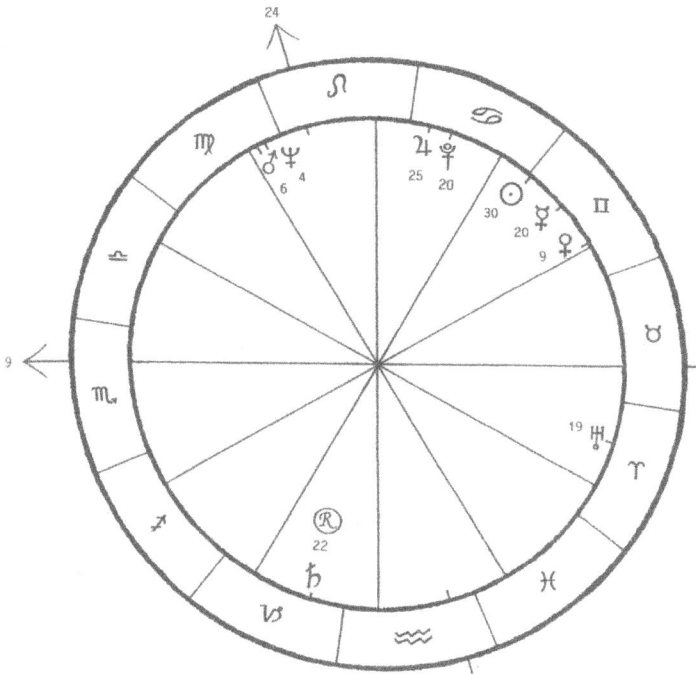

Birthchart of David Oliver

In powerful opposition to Saturn is the conjunction of Pluto with Jupiter. Pluto — the collective time factor — will continually be stirring Jupiter — the individual soul — to seek the new horizons promised by the ninth house which they both occupy, but the process will always be under scrutiny by the individual Saturnian time factor, directed inwards. It can imply action or surrender, dependent upon the intuitive acceptability of those factors currently presenting themselves to the soul.

181

The degree and its symbol is particularly significant in this case, for not only is Saturn strongly placed in the unconscious area of the chart, but the ephemeris for the year in question tells us that this planet was retrograde at the time of birth. It indicates a surrendering of outer defences, whilst all the resistance-building power symbolized by Saturn is concentrated instead on fortifying the inner — on the creation of invulnerability within the soul. As soul-growth proceeds through the threefold cycle and its successive trigger points, changes will occur and barriers will be broached spontaneously, accompanied in all probability by deep-rooted upheavals. And the fact that Saturn is in its "home territory" of Capricorn and, what is more, within the third house — concerned with one's relationship with the environment — suggests that all these upheavals will have a truly practical manifestation, involving an actual change of occupation, character and milieu.

The conjunction of Mars with Neptune implies a tremendous source of energy directed towards the world of spirit. Interpreted at one level, it implies unusual sex impulses, and the sextile aspect of these two planets with the ascendant stresses the creative nature of this activity, whether normally seen as high or low. The same conjunction is in sesquiquadrate aspect with Saturn, stressing an intuitive awareness of the *inner* importance of both spheres of activity. Its nonagon aspect with Jupiter connects these factors creatively and firmly with the subject's personal soul; its semi-square aspect with Pluto brings assurance that such activities and their outcome will take a positively conscious form. Linked with this conjunction too are the two adjacent aspects of the Sun, quintile with Mars and sextile with Neptune. They hint at a certain willingness to submit to Martian passions creatively to a higher purpose.

The same conjunction of Mars with Neptune in 135° aspect with both Uranus and Saturn forms a perfect sesquiquadrate triangle, and the transitted Pluto adds its weight to this unusual combination. It implies that these creative factors, normally unconscious, will always be present within the subject's awareness.

The opposition of Saturn to Pluto, whilst Pluto itself is in conjunction with Jupiter in the ninth house (concerned with projection of the individual to new horizons), and their mutual 90° square with Uranus, completes a T-square. There will certainly always be tremendous inner tension between the factors thus symbolized: the personal soul as Jupiter, triggered by Pluto, opposed by Saturn, vying with the determined pull of an Arien Uranus in the emotional area of the chart — the tantalizing flow of those "images of the collective unconscious". At 25 years of age, when the subject's point of self reached the point of "awareness of limitations" and, coming into opposition to Uranus, completed the Grand Cross, this awareness was very real. Almost inevitably, in the absence of practical fulfilment, he experienced a period of deep depression.

Rebirth in a new cycle

If we follow the point of self to the ascendant, and thus to the completion of the first cycle of houses at 28 years of age, plotting the planetary transits for the same date we uncover an outstandingly important phase in the subject's life, All transitted planets were now in the eastern hemisphere. Neptune had arrived in exact conjunction with the radical ascendant, this planet and the point of self together entering the first house of "new found freedom". It signalled the end of the destructively depressive period, and heralded a dramatic awakening of soul-consciousness. At the completion of the ancestral cycle it represented a fulfilment of the twelfth house with its accent on self-abnegation, and a new "coming to awareness" of the self.

Transitted Pluto was now in conjunction with radical or birthpoint Mars (and therefore also with Neptune), and in smoothly sextile aspect with the ascendant. As we have already noted, Pluto was also in sesquiquadrate aspect with both Saturn and Uranus, as though to strengthen the newly inspired surge of an individual soul towards its collective goal. Transitted Saturn has completed its full revolution and returned to Capricorn at the very cusp of the third house, to form an exact trine with transitted Pluto and birthpoint Mars and Neptune, and a sextile aspect with the ascendant. A transitting conjunction of Mars and Jupiter with their powerful intuitional undercurrent operating in the second house, was in nonagon aspect to the ascendant, whilst the transitting Uranus was in near conjunction with the objective-indicating MC in the south-eastern, thinking area of the chart. With Neptune on the ascendant to symbolize a newly discovered ocean of creative depths, the second, soul-navigated cycle had begun, the course set through a rhythmic swell of both sexual and spiritual impulses. Matters that had long remained hidden in the receptacle of the soul came openly to the surface to form a new centre of gravity.

All this strangeness was plainly leading towards a new-found identity that would have reality for the subject. If we follow the transitting point of self to the appropriate point (at thirty-five years of age) we can find this state of affairs clearly symbolized. The transitting planets have all reached remarkable positions in their relationships to each other, to the birth chart, and in the symbols of their respective degrees. There is a balance now between the four quarters of the chart.

In the south-eastern area characterized by the thinking process, Pluto is in close conjunction with Uranus. The subject's objective thoughts seem at last to be able to explore the mystic collective passions! In the north-eastern area of intuition, Neptune symbolizes a "new-found freedom" for truly human instincts, and the instinctually-based *inner* feelings. In the north-western area, the physically-oriented timekeeper Saturn is now based in emotion. In the south-western area of sensation are Jupiter and Mars, representing the individual soul and the passions through which it normally expresses itself, now able to take part jointly in physical phenomena which have originated somewhere beyond the will, that is, in "miraculous movements" instigated by the awakened soul.

As a precursor of this tangible evidence of spiritual reality, inevitably, the septile aspect of death of the base passions and the consequent opening of the soul to receive quickening impulses into the inner self, Pluto (degree symbol now: *A volcano suddenly erupts*), and Uranus (in the adjacent degree: *A spiritualist medium is holding a seance*) together are in exact septile aspect with Jupiter at birthpoint — with the individual soul, *as it was.* Simultaneously the point of self comes into septile aspect with the transitted Saturn (with a degree of cyclic fulfilment: *A giant face has been carved into a mountain*). The death suggested by the septile aspect marks the completion of one stage of striving, the death of the old, and the attainment of a new level of being beyond the merely material considerations.

The birthpoint MC, meanwhile, is in semi-quintile aspect with transitted Jupiter (degree symbol: *An upper class girl marries a working class boy*, representing the union of outer male "mind" and inner female "anima", and the permanent union of a "dead" ego with the individual soul). The MC is also in nonagon aspect with transitted Mars, on the degree symbolized: *A baby lies chuckling on a bright yellow blanket.* The common passions, the desires considered as an independent entity, feeling that their humanity has at last taken tangible form, supported as it were by the (spiritually yellow) animal life forces beneath them, delight in their strange new experience. Their role is now that of passively amused onlooker, as Neptunian waves of collective "passions" pour in to rejuvenate the inner self and establish its place within the collective realm of mankind.

Neptune is now in agreeable sextile aspect with the transitted Pluto-Uranus conjunction, and is retrograde in its degree, within the Scorpionic span of valuation, which has the symbol: *A woman opens a white gate leading from the forest.* This planet's retrogression means that there is no massive shock to the system. The process of receiving a "new identity", though triggered inwardly instantaneously, will probably be at first barely perceptible, only gradually, week by week, coming to the fully involved awareness of heart and mind.

Living the inner life

Retrogression of one or two planets in a birth chart may imply a comparatively slight or subtle peculiarity of the psyche, but in cases where most or all of the planets are caught "running backwards" at the time of birth, they will symbolize a far more deeply felt state of affairs. In David Oliver's chart only Saturn was retrograde, as was the case with Dane Rudhyar. Saturn retrograde, being symbolic of a powerful inner life, is a characteristic feature in the birth charts of those tending towards mysticism, and almost inevitably it occurs in the two ensuing birth charts also.

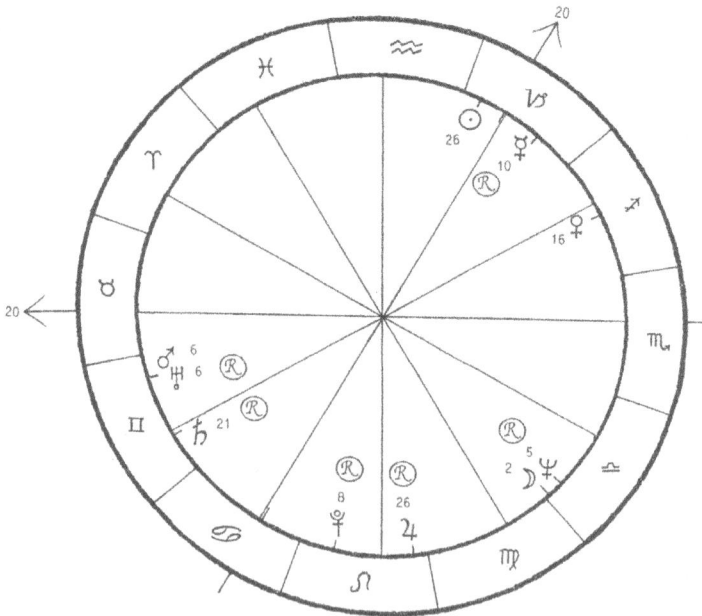

Birthchart of Robert Foster

Oliver's retrograde Saturn, symbolically, was immensely strengthened by its powerful placing on his chart. At Robert Foster's birth, not only was Saturn retrograde, but Jupiter, Neptune and Pluto were retrograde too. Of the fast-moving planets only Mercury was retrograde, which may help to express his introverted style of thinking, strengthened by the Moon's position at the time of birth, *within* the Earth's orbit of the Sun.

The first thing one cannot help but notice about Robert Foster's chart is the fact that all the slow-moving planets are situated below the horizon, as though to shade themselves from the light and heat of publicity. The individual soul, as Jupiter, and the collective soul, as Neptune, empowered as it were by its sextile aspect with Pluto, are gathered in the emotional zone; Mars, as representative of the individual passions, their mutual function to be triggered by nearby Saturn — the subject's Capricornian ruling planet — in the intuitional area of the chart. All this seems to add up to a most unusual personality.

Recalling that all the outer planets except Mars were retrograde at the time of birth we can readily understand that the life-qualities of this man differ widely from those of the majority, and that he is one who for the most part lives the "inner life". And when we refer to the degree symbol for his Sun in 296°: *A luminous sprite dances on the mist of a waterfall,* and that for his Taurean ascendant in 50°: *Wispy clouds like streamers spread across the sky,* we realize that the personality which we have uncovered has a particularly insubstantial, or non-material quality, and at the same time a firm grip on practical, material realities — in fact, we could say, a thoroughly enigmatic character.

People who know Robert Foster personally would say that he is not an easy man to pin down; he can see the pin coming and dodge it with ease. However there is a strong balancing trait running contrary to this trend, perhaps reflected here by the fact that Mars is direct (*An oil platform is drilling through the night —* he is a confirmed night-owl!) and so is Venus, opposing it in the seventh house with Mercury retrograde in the eighth house. He has in fact a keenly practical mind for technology, engineering and logistics, is personally daring, well able to envisage profitable enterprises, equip them, and put them into successful practice.

Birth chart Sun, the integrating principle, is near the MC, implying that Robert's main objective in life is to become "whole", a "better person". The fact that the Sun is in quintile aspect with the ascendant shows that he will always be well aware of this driving inner need, or psychological direction. But there is no hint, either in the chart or in the man, of any strengthening of the ego that one might normally associate with ambition in any direction. Mars is in exact conjunction with retrograde Uranus, implying that he is in direct touch with his own inner feelings. Uranus is also in parallel declination with the retrograde Saturn, which confirms the inner contact but seems to ensure that he will always keep such matters private. The Mars-Uranus conjunction is in sesquiquadrate aspect with the MC, adding the strength of objectivity to this intention, in trine with retrograde Neptune and sextile with retrograde Pluto. We can be sure that this unusual contact with matters that normally belong to the collective unconscious takes place easily and naturally, and is not, as sometimes happens, a source of neurosis or paranoia. At the expense, some might say, of outgoing personality, the whole chart suggests the building up from childhood of a powerful inner strength. On this inner level Robert Foster will always be in creative harmony with fellow seekers after truth, though he would be unlikely to express this as a fact.

Saturn retrograde in the second house stresses the conscious "keeping to oneself" of finely developed inner factors. Saturn is in sextile aspect with Jupiter, retrograde here in the fourth house of new spiritual growth, and this implies that Robert's most creative activities will be accomplished, not by striving, but by calm acceptance and submission to the quiet but insistent voice of the inner. The few other aspects in the chart all seem to point in the same direction. Jupiter and Neptune are in nonagon relationship, suggesting their creative cooperation and their mutual assimilation by the inner self in an appropriate, completely non-egoistical way. The MC too is in bi-quintile aspect with Jupiter as though to ensure that the subject's inner and outer objectives are as one — growth, harmony, and progress.

An important discovery

It seems a simple enough discovery to make: the fact that truly creative, spiritual activities are to be accomplished, not by strength of will, but by apparent weakness — by strength of submission to fine non-zodiacal life forces, by allowing oneself to be open and receptive to the possibility of experiencing them. But as it is certainly one of the most important discoveries that a person can make, it would be as well to explore the nature of "will", in terms of astrology and the inner self. "Will" can indeed achieve all sorts of things within the bounds of the zodiac, but it *cannot* serve to approach such finer forms of life as may lie beyond. The will, in short, belongs to the personality; conscious non-will belongs to the inner self. By the use of will the outer planets, in symbolic terms, can be seen to function on an utterly impersonal basis. Their principles can be said to rule whole races, nations, and unruly mobs. Unwilled, however, these same outer planets, still in symbolic terms, have the quality of plotting or recording the progress of the inner self. They represent not only the individual having become collective, but also the collective having become individual.

The passions or desires that comprise the nature of the zodiac itself, though instinctively expressed, form the foundation, the driving force of "will". Passion there is a-plenty. Allowing a state of non-passion to take over the innermost soul can be possible only to the extent that the personal external passions are allowed to subside. But words of course can be misleading, and the word "passion" has different meanings for different people. For Christians it carries the implication of suffering, as in Christ's passion leading up to his death on the cross. In everyday language it has come to mean intensity or strongly expressed emotions, and is often used purely in the sense of sexual attraction. I am using the word here not in any dramatic or particularly vehement sense but in the sense of a focus of everyday feeling, wanting, or desiring.

In this sense of "wanting", the passions and all earthly feelings and desires are certainly connected with the instinctual guiding forces described in chapter two: the "wants" or needs of animals and plants. The mineral or material life forces can be said to give rise in humans to the passion of greed, an exaggeration of "wanting". In a sense, they work through the "gathering" impulse, the accumulation of matter by the force of gravity. The animal life forces can be said to give rise to the everyday human passions of desire, pride and sensual enjoyment, bodily comfort and sexual gratification. In the same way the plant life forces can be said to give rise, through their continual competitive striving, to the human characteristics of arrogance, selfishness, callousness, and sheer bad temper, beside determination and persistence — desirable qualities for the successful entrepreneur. The natural human life forces too give rise to our passion for observation and our urge to acquire knowledge, to take charge of situations and get things organized.

The ups and downs of passion

These four passions — observation, which in its most poisitive form becomes "sincerity"; desire, which can become "submission"; arrogance, which can become "patience"; and greed, which in its most positive form can become "faith" — these four can combine to give a fifth, this time the warm and well-directed passion of love. Being *collective* by nature, it has to be completely unselfish. "Love" vindicates the coarser individual passions because, although it is of their nature, it symbolizes the influence of higher life forces not normally to be felt. In this sense, it is the only "spiritual" influence that can readily be experienced, even by insensitive souls. This coming together of the passions may also be expressed as compassion — the super-passion that by its very nature cannot be used in a self-seeking way.

The sensitive areas of the psyche where the binding power of the zodiac has become focused into a significant passion, can be plotted as a personal mandala at points 72° apart, forming the basis of the quintile aspects on the birth chart. These are not in any sense fixed points on a dial; their positions will alter continually within the same ratio, depending on the subject's current centre of psychic gravity. In the ideal human being, perhaps, "compassion" could be said to correspond to the Sun on his or her chart. In this way, by taking the place of the usual principle of "objectivity", by occupying the niche usually occupied by disunited passions, it will symbolize the cancellation of the driving power of these passions, and indicate possibilities that should prove wholly natural and beneficial for that person.

Passions cannot be called "bad". Used in moderation, they are a normal and necessary adjunct for a full life. It is only when the whole of a person's attention becomes focused on an objective, when the full force of the passions are directed towards a particular aim, that they take on a sinister significance. It happens very noticeably during sporting occasions where there is a large public following. The person who uses passions in this way, hoping to achieve their desire, in a sense is practising magic, and magic is inimical to spiritual growth.

Linked, the points of 72° intervals plotted within a circle take the form of a pentagram — an ancient symbol of magical intent. The coming together of the passions into unified compassion may also be signified by the pentagram, but in this case the action will have taken place without intent. Compassion simply cannot be applied to deliberate or selfish ends! The contributory passions will effectively have been cancelled out, and the person whose passions are gathered in this involuntary way can never be called a magician or a witch. The two types of focusing, in the one case submissive and in the other case wilful, exemplify the irreconcilable difference between a prophet and a sorceror, between the spiritual and the material, between the potentially divine and the potentially satanic.

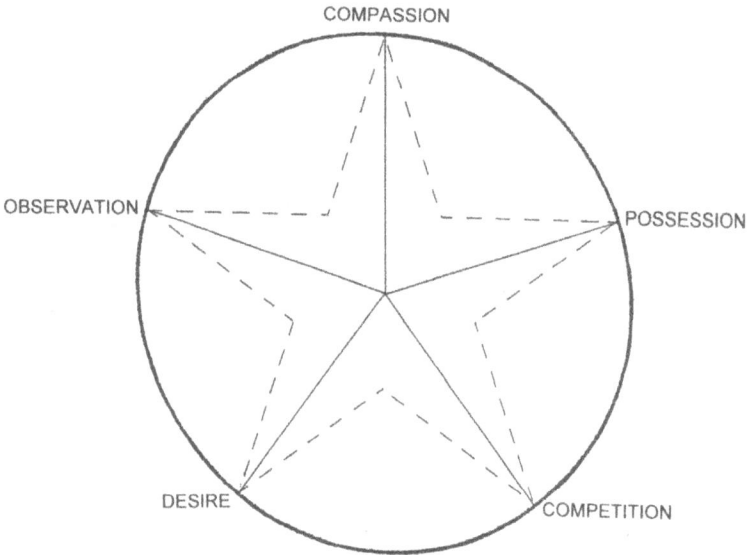

The Quintile Aspects — The Basic Passions of Humanity

The terms black magic and white magic (also, but scarcely remembered, red magic and yellow magic), originally came about because the five passions traditionally have colours attributed to them. The passion for observation associated with the human life forces is called white; the passion for carnal desire on the animal level is called yellow; the passion for aggressive arrogance on the plant level is called red; and the passion for possession on the material level is called black. When they come together in even proportions, these four basic colours make the composite colour brown, and this is the colour traditionally ascribed to the fifth and highest passion: compassion, or love.

Again, the best way to appreciate the astrological symbolism of this, is to apply it to one's own chart, using the mundane symbols of the zodiac degrees. And once again, too, let us take David Oliver's chart and analyse the potentially changing patterns of his desires. Let us first assume that he is not given to focusing his passions too strongly along any particular channel of desire. Let us suppose that he is reasonably patient, sincere, easy-going, and uses his power of will for normal, everyday purposes. He has genuine faith in forces greater than himself, and is not one to stir up supernatural powers, or try to attain his ambitions by means of the occult.

"Brown" compassion, then, we take to refer to his Sun degree at the close of Gemini on 90°. If he is fortunate enough to feel true love he will express it in the way normal for his own character hinted at by the symbol for that degree. Forward 72°, the "white" human passion of observation will function normally as symbolized for 162°: *An Indian groom gently lifts his bride's veil,* This seems to imply a gentle, benevolent urge to uncover natural mysteries, to look beneath the veil or ritual and see things as they really are. It seems to imply a readiness to see beauty in ordinary things; to accept characteristics other than his own; to treat life with reverence and people with kindness. It suggests that the civilizing human influence is being put to good use during the normal course of events.

72° on again, the "yellow" passion of animal desires will function mainly through 234°, where the appropriate symbol reads: *Reassured, citizens leave a public enquiry.* Here again, the emphasis is on finding out how things really are. The subject will probably put his own desires to the test of public approval before putting them into practice. He won't put on an act. He may perhaps see nothing wrong in lusty desires, but they will at least be submitted first to the test of his own judgment. He will weigh them intelligently, and make sure they are justified.

Another 72° gives us the "red" plant world passion of arrogance at 306°. The symbol for this reads: *A parish priest conducts a simple service alone.* This suggests that, although the subject may feel aggression, it will probably be applied to himself, and in private. Arrogance will scarcely make an appearance outside the privacy of his own mind, and seldom directed at others. He may well feel superior in a quiet way, taking pride in his ability to withdraw to his own private "service" within. No-one would be better able to conduct that service than a lone priest, content with his own company and his own sense of sufficiency. If that brand of superiority can be called arrogance, at least outsiders would be unlikely to take offence!

To complete the five points of the pentagram, 72° on brings us to 18°, and the "black" passion representing the desire for possessions. The symbol reads: *An empty hammock swings between two trees.* There will always be symbols within a symbol. The trees in this case could represent the plant life forces, and the hammock the forces of materiality. Most materially-oriented souls have severed all contact with the subtle life forces above them, but in this case the subject is still as comfortable as might be, without a hampering accumulation of wealth. The hammock suggests that he sees no need to sleep rough on the rocky floor of humanity's spiritual descent. He seems to be making good use of the lower forces without actually falling under their sway. This is hardly greed at all!

A change of orientation

So it seems that the subject is likely to possess a tranquil aura — a gentle person, whose lower passions are readily disengaged. But now let us suppose that this same subject has taken an interest in modifying his own passions, determining to concentrate them of his own will and create compassion for himself. The ruling passion of his wish will now occupy his centre of objectivity.

This objective passion will not belong to the Sun degree, because the astrological Sun speaks of integration, and thus potentially at least should represent the brown passion only. The ruling passion of a person with intent will correspond with the degree of midheaven, the personal zenith of the MC — the current objective, however selfless it may seem to be, of the individual.

But the ruling passion of the MC cannot be the brown passion of love — it would not be possible, because compassion cannot be *held* as an objective. It is involuntary. As soon as an objective comes into being, the passion of wanting, desiring, using, or studying that objective will occupy the focus. Though it may seem at first sight laudable, an ambition to use inner strength, and to develop the power of will to assist even the most worthy of human causes, inevitably transfers the white passion to the individual's objective degree. This is "white magic". The passion itself, through observation and meaningful intent, will occupy the peak of the conscious mind and become the factor by which the world is judged, the basis for reaction. By this simple change of focus, the subject will have become a very different person: more successful, perhaps, certainly more sophisticated or complicated, but farther away from the possibility of compassion.

So the human passion of observation is now set on the MC at 144° with the symbol: *An Indian fakir, unwashed and ragged.* Symbols can rarely be taken literally, but in this case a literal interpretation may be near the truth. If it is to work at all, human "magic" must be accompanied by an ascetic sense of striving in a physical way, a strengthening of the will, and perhaps a hint of the contemptuous superiority that expertise in occult matters is liable to bring. The fakir represents the lowest of the "ways", for his work involves purely physical effort to bring about magical results. In the fakir's own eyes, his efforts will be aimed at producing spiritual results, but it is difficult to see how successive layers of spiritual quality can be stirred from below in this way, let alone transcended, working as he does from the bottom of the heap. This is the physical basis of willpower, this degree of the fakir, and this would be the basis from which David Oliver would be constrained to operate, if he possessed determination of this type. As a white magician, this is the manner in which the learning, observing function will operate in his inner nature — even though his purpose may be "good", he will be heedless even of normal ethical patterns of behaviour. He will be looking at everything in relation to its occult potential.

A further 72° sees the yellow passion of animal desire at 216°: *With the lure of gold, prospectors throng the wilderness.* This is in striking contrast to the previous "animal degree", with its accent on reason, weighing, balancing, considering all sides of an argument, and arriving at a truthfully fair solution. With the present symbol there is no consideration of conflicting points of view, no allowance for the weaknesses or needs of others. His instinctive "animal wants" will now be motivated solely by the possibility of personal gain, by the forceful attitude of "me first". His "animal nature" will also, it seems, have acquired a strongly materialistic flavour, grabbing what it can, and elbowing others out of the way. When he sees the object of his desires, like a gold-rush prospector Oliver will stake his claim and guard it fiercely, keeping competitors at bay by whatever means are at hand.

Another interval of 72° registers the red plant force passion of arrogant competition at 288°, with the symbol: *A warship, flying the flag on her maiden voyage.* Plainly, Oliver will have become a person who looks for trouble, making a display of strength when he thinks it politic to do so, torpedoing or shooting down, protecting his own and his family's interests irrespective of the well-being or dignity of other mortals. The implication is always of triumph within the confines, if not of self and family alone, then of his own kind, class, race, or nation.

The next 72° places the black passion of acquisitive greed at 360°, with the symbol: *A giant face has been carved into the side of a mountain.* This is really a frightening symbol of material lust for possession! The culminating degree of the zodiac, it represents the materialization of an abstract concept. There could be few symbols so appropriate for material ambition, and for the ambitions of magic — the intention to bring all human aspiration to tangible reality through the medium of the passions.

Through Oliver's hypothetical orientation towards white magic, the culminating point of his brown passion will have moved on to 72°, with its symbol: *A slave girl confronts her mistress boldly.* It is rather sad, because the passions cannot really come together under the present pattern. The symbol is split between mastery and slavery, and such flashes of compassion as the subject may experience are liable to be of a "schizoid" nature; the results will not be entirely altruistic. Dominance and submission, suppression and rebellion, arrogant self-assurance and hopelessly misplaced ambition; these are the conflicts that could emerge. Through challenging forces greater than himself his own soul will be held captive, as the slave of those forces. He who wins by magic is also the loser. By taking into himself and concentrating influences that are normally well diffused and not all-compelling, he is building up a karmic shell that can only reduce the possibility of achieving his true spiritual potential.

Fortunately, David Oliver has managed to avoid such a fate and, I am sure, would be unlikely consciously to practice magic, black or white; but he would probably be the first to admit that his passions rarely "come together" to form selfless love. It is something of which we can all experience a foretaste, but permanent "compassion" can come about only when the individual has transcended the spiritual level of "ordinary" humans.

I know of only one man who not only surpassed this level during his lifetime but actually lived most of his long life as a whole person within the highest sphere possible for humans on Earth. He was almost certainly the only person in recent centuries to have had this happen — for it was not brought about by his own willing — and this was Muhammad Subuh Sumohadiwidjojo, the founder of the spiritual organisation known as *Susila Budhi Dharma,* or Subud.

His birth chart certainly is full of implications. Pluto is just below the horizon in the 18th degree of his rising sign, with its symbol: *Inscrutable easterners visit the west.* It could be said to symbolize the unwilled trigger mechanism that always accompanied him during his life. In the ascendant too, within the intuitive zone beneath the surface of self-will, Neptune is in near conjunction with the Sun.

197

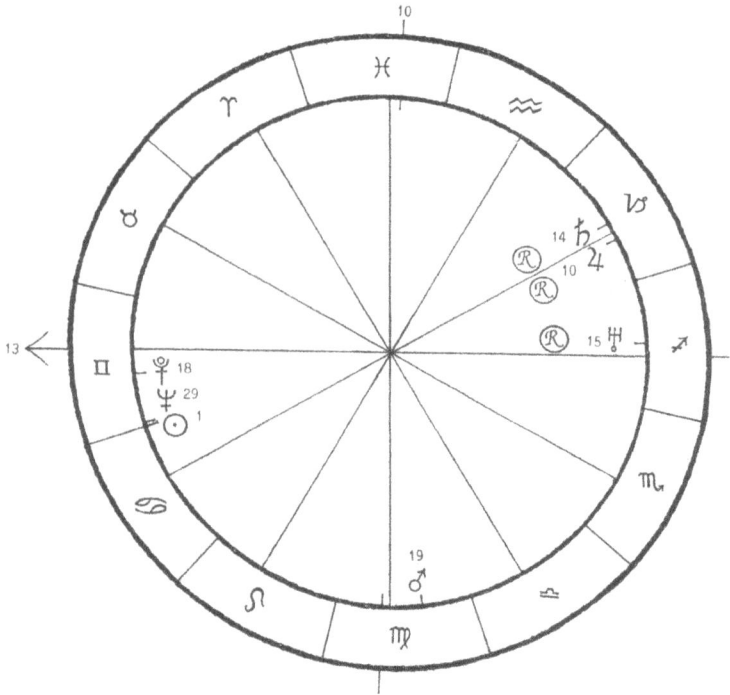

Birth date	22 June 1901	Sidereal Time noon GMT	5 55 56
Birth place	Nr. Semarang	Interval from noon pm +	9 38 00
Latitude	7° 22' S		15 33 56
Longitude	110° 30' E		
		Accel. On Interval pm +	1 36
Birth time as given	5 00 00 am	ST Greenwich at birth	15 35 32
Local Mean Time E+	7 22 00	Longitude equiv. E +	7 22 00
Greenwich Mean Time	9 38 00 pm	Local ST at birth	22 57 32
Date at Greenwich	21 June 1901	Adjust S hemisphere	12 00 00
			34 57 32
		Less 24 hours	10 57 32

Birthchart of Muhammad Subuh Sumohadiwidjojo

Wholly spiritual

The degree symbol for Neptune at 89°(Gemini 29°) suggests the commencement of a new era: *Song birds herald the arrival of spring*. Following the horizon to the west we see that Uranus is just above the descendant, at the tangible point of "giving out" to others — the practical receiving point for us ordinary mortals. Perhaps this symbolizes the common experience of those who came into personal contact with Muhammad Subuh: personal passions combined to produce love, and the unwilled flow of "collective passions", ancient wisdoms channelled directly from their source. Pluto and Uranus, you will see, are in opposition, and exactly square with this aspect, forming a T-square. Mars (with its symbol: *An Olympic swimming event is under way*) stands alone near the IC, in the fourth house of new spiritual growth. From this one might assume that individual passions would not, or could not be used assertively, in the outer sense. The combination of aspects suggests (and in retrospect I can confirm) that the potential outflow of collective contents would be actualized, and would really be put into practical effect.

All three planets to the west, Uranus, Jupiter and Saturn, were retrograde at birth; Saturn — as we might have expected — suggesting the construction of a powerful inner nature, though it might be at the expense of the worldly ego. All the influence brought to bear on others by Muhammad Subuh during his lifetime was related to the inner reality. Retrograde Saturn and retrograde Jupiter are in conjunction, as though to strengthen and confirm the idea of non-personal inner power. Jupiter is near the final cusp of the seventh house, representing realization to the full extent of unity at the personal level, whilst Saturn is just beyond the cusp and into the eighth house, at the beginning of shared resources. In this position it seems to suggest the unselfish use of material possessions, the idea of mutually cooperative enterprise. Uranus, Saturn and Jupiter are in conjunction to the south, all three in opposition to Neptune in the north. Evidently the personal soul was potentially in tune with the collective passions; but as yet, at birth,

199

as a reflection in the natal chart, the collective soul looked on, as it were, without taking part.

Mars you will see is running direct, and so is Neptune, symbolizing the ability of Pak Subuh to retain his conventional religion (he was what I would call a devoutly benign Muslim with a flavouring of Javan Hinduism) with most (but not all) of its traditional rituals, practiced from within, governed directly by the movements of the soul. He accepted the purpose of religion as an important "comforter" for the heart — for the outer feelings. Although, probably above all men, he had access to the ultimate spiritual reality, without a shred of hypocrisy, he followed the accepted religion of his own cultural background and recommended others to follow their own respective religions, whatever they may be. Had he been the sort of person symbolized by Neptune running retrograde at birth, it seems doubtful to me whether he would have been able to do this with sincerity.

During his twenty-fifth year, Muhammad Subuh spontaneously received contact with the Holy Spirit. Planets transitted to this year on his chart show that the birthpoint MC came into septile aspect with Jupiter to the west. Neptune had moved into septile aspect with the Sun. The incident signalled the death of his personal, everyday passions, and plainly, his normal lifestyle had to be abandoned. Transitted Pluto had come into exact trine with the MC, and stood in opposition to the Saturn-Jupiter conjunction (especially so with regard to Jupiter). Transitted Saturn too was in trine with the MC, and transitted Uranus had come into quintile aspect with Saturn and Jupiter.

Muhammad Subuh's prolonged receiving of divine influences (and which you could say resulted in the death of what most people would think of as "personality") culminated at the close of the first and the commencement of the second twenty-eight year cycle. By this time, transitting Jupiter had come into septile aspect with the birthpoint MC again, but this time to the *east*. Jupiter was also septile to the birthpoint conjunction of Sun and Neptune. Transitting Pluto, which had barely moved during this three-year period, was still in opposition to the Saturn-Jupiter conjunction, this time more particularly with regard to Saturn. Transitted Saturn had come into exact conjunction with birthpoint Uranus, and thus in opposition to birthpoint Pluto.

This period marked the completion of Muhammad Subuh's passage through that part of the three-fold cycle summarized as "awareness of limitations". In doing so it marked the beginning of his great purpose, the "new-found freedom" of his first rebirth, again into the first house, and the freedom or ability to pass on the divine contact that he had received to the whole of mankind — to as many as would seek it. This was the foundation of *Susila Budhi Dharma*, the international organization better known by the acronym Subud. A detailed study of planetary transits during this period will demonstrate how "compassion" set on a Sun sign operates. The reappearance of transitting Saturn at the point of conjunction with Uranus and its opposition to Pluto, saw Pak Subuh and his spiritual influence travelling to the west, fulfilling the promise of his birth chart.

Saturn's next return to conjoin with natal Uranus coincided with the death of this world-teacher at the age of eighty-six. The end of one cycle marks the beginning of another. Transitted Jupiter had now arrived in septile aspect with birth point Pluto, and death this time was not merely the death of earthly passions. But transitting Pluto was displaying harmonious, creative aspects all round. It was in trine with the birthpoint MC and bi-quintile with birthpoint Uranus. Transitting Uranus reached the central point in opposition to birthpoint Pluto, Neptune, and the Sun, falling within the orb of all three.

Transitting Mars, square with transitting Jupiter, was in semi-quintile aspect with birthpoint Pluto. In parallel declination Neptune, Uranus and Saturn were in conjunction to the south, opposing Mars to the north, the last of earthly passions finally discarded. The inner self of Muhammad Subuh had become one with the world beyond the zodiac, blazing a trail, some might say, for the rest of us to follow.

I hope these example charts will have pointed out traits which may be thought to carry spiritual significance. When casting one's own horoscope with the inner self in mind, the non-material nature of synchronicity is such that one's approach does not *need* mathematical precision. Synchronicity displayed by the movements of the Sun and the planets against the background of the Zodiac can be a confirmation for us, not of clever ideas, but of sensitive inner feelings. If the need to contact the soul is felt at this time, if we truly feel the need to bring about the soul's awakening and emergence into the light of consciousness through its introduction to spirit, if this is our sincere wish, the moment of realization may be near. This reality, this contact with divine influences, can be ours. It is our newly emerging birthright.

CHAPTER 8

Influences from beyond the zodiac

Our approach to matters of the soul and the inner self has so far been symbolic, necessarily so, and even the phrase "beyond the zodiac" is merely a symbol. It is difficult to describe the non-material in material terms, The zodiac itself, in our symbolism, is taken to represent the bounds of materiality which, in surrounding our solar system, surrounds us all. As well as our physical being and our everyday passions, the zodiac also has to include the so-called occult, "that which is hidden", representing the subtle side of the world of passions; strange, magical realms which many have found seductively alluring.

The phrase "beyond the zodiac", therefore, let it be clear, is taken to symbolize, not the occult, but that unknown and unlimited state of being which lies beyond the occult and beyond collective mortality. Any out-of-the-ordinary experiences may be described as "spiritual", and many have claimed familiarity with this vast spiritual field; but few indeed are those who would claim to understand it. Certainly, aspects of it can be experienced, so perhaps it is true to say that it can be known; it is not "hidden" like the occult. But the field of spirit cannot really be understood by human minds, simply because our intellectual and emotional understanding cannot extend beyond the state of materiality in which we live.

I suppose most thoughtful people would maintain that, in the final analysis, all human experience must take place within, and therefore be dependent upon, the mind. Even the most abstract of matters, one might suppose, coming lightly to awareness, could be received and understood only by the receptive

203

mind itself. Even those who normally tend to rely on their emotional feelings as their main vehicle for expression would probably agree with this.

But is this the whole truth of the matter? The brain may be the seat of knowledge, but is it the seat of wisdom? You do not even have to think about something in order to know it, to be aware of it. We can safely assume, I think, that the "whole person" must have a spiritual, non-material dimension. It is difficult to understand what personal wholeness can mean. As we all know, the separate parts of almost anything can be analyzed and thereby understood. "Wholes", on the other hand, cannot be analysed in order to understand them, or they will no longer be wholes; they can only be accepted on trust, in their entirety. There is no real place for logic in the process of spiritual regeneration. Wholeness, it seems, calls for symbolic representation in order for it to be grasped by the mind — if, indeed, there is a necessity for it to be grasped. The use of symbols can initiate the process and lead the way, but once the whole has been accepted as such, the time for symbolism will have passed. Astrology of the inner self should be leading towards something that cannot, in fact, be grasped by the understanding. In the way of really effective symbols, therefore, it is leading towards its own death. It and the truth it represents can only be experienced in that light.

Within the orbit of Saturn — within the symbolic bounds, that is, of mortality — it may reasonably be said that mind is the sole arbiter of human knowledge. But experience may confirm that this apparently self-evident truth is not really true. What we usually call "mind" is not the be-all and end-all; there is very different seat of consciousness that once realized can be operative whilst remaining quite detached from the mind, detached from thought, from sensation, from feeling, and even from intuition. When this type of awareness comes into being, our familiar psychic functions can only stand aside quietly, watching, listening, and finally accepting as a whole verifiable experience, that which cannot be understood by the everyday tools of understanding.

This may seem out of keeping with the New Age ethos of self-help, quick-fix, personal growth. Many are convinced that they have found an inner guiding light, and in following it have experienced an outward change that may be beneficial. But as a rule these apparently positive results turn out to belong to the personality alone: relaxation; relief from tensions; a sense of control; strengthening of the will. Such changes cannot stir the soul to life. For this to happen, the intervention of some benign power from beyond our own material sphere is essential: a spark, an unknown enzyme, the catalyst that will start a new reaction; a seed that will germinate within the soul, and slowly take root.

The wheel of becoming

The fate of the Earth, it is said, is death; the cycle of seasons, death and rebirth, running its continuous course. Through the power of nature, indeed, the world is in a state of constant regeneration. The personal mandala of the birth chart, trapped as it were within the surrounding zodiac of nature by the very fact of personal birth — the allegorical Buddhist Wheel of Becoming — symbolizes the fate of its native incumbent. Is that personal fate too a seemingly endless cycle of death and rebirth? There are some who treasure the idea of reincarnation as a reassurance, a promise, a justification for hard times in this life. Others think of it as a cruel fate to be avoided. Plainly, a fate of "becoming" should lead to a destiny of wholeness, an eventual state of having arrived. Good or bad, symbolic idea or hard fact, reincarnation cannot be our true destiny. But in symbolic terms certainly it is the fate of souls who have not reached awareness: animals, plants, and all those whose lives fall under the harsh laws of nature and of Saturn.

Saturn, or the principle of time, however, need not be seen as a negative force bringing death and suffering to the individual. A more positive outlook may be less concerned with individuality, and will lead us to accept the collective principle of time as a creative force, leading to increased awareness — the awareness of possibilities for the future other than merely the end of life. Our attitude need not involve defiance in the face of inevitability. It should be more a matter of compliance, of surrender; inner expansion involves submission to the creative moment, the moment made whole by spirit. The *idea* of wholeness grows with a cycle of moments, culminating in a single moment of truth which can render the zodiac irrelevant. Wholeness embraces equally that which is above, below, and on either side. "Wholeness" must mean just that; it has to involve not only the self but relationships with others as well. The whole self has to include the full complement both of individual and of collective elements.

Obviously, there is no escape from death. But death, to be humanly meaningful, should be conscious and aware of itself. We know that, having been opened to receive spiritual influences, the soul seems obliged to experience something very like death during physical life, sometimes repeatedly, as its personal contents — its passions — are replaced by finer influences. Indeed, all changes for the better that take place in the spiritual world are obliged to do so through the process of death. Many who search for a way through the oppressive barrier of the instinctual lower life forces have hoped to find a method of change and renewal that does not also involve dying. The great religions of the world give us the answer, in one form or another: only the soul that is filled with spirit — simultaneously "son of man" and "child of God" — is able to transcend death. But whether these great religions still contain the spirit introduced by their founders, in this day and age, is surely a matter of some doubt.

We all know the conscious mind, with its thinking and theorizing. Many too know of the unconscious mind, with its apprehension and instinctive awareness. But many people who wish to do so may now experience the awakening of their soul, and discover how thoughts and feelings may be "received" in consciousness aside from the mind; how physical movements may be "received" in consciousness aside from the normal mechanisms of the body. The "inner self" is a broad and seemingly vague term, but it expresses or implies inner creativity. At soul level, creativity

206

is not a matter of the will; the decision, the impetus, reaches the soul from within; it is a matter of "receiving". To actually experience this is to commence a new cycle, this time on an ever-rising spiral, growing from a garden in which the soul itself is the germinating seed, experiencing strange new growth as it expands. It will grow silently, developing slowly in the darkness, before finally bursting into the symbolic light of day as the spiral of self thrusts through the substance of the zodiac.

Inevitably, we run into the old religious debate about "free will", and it may indeed be our will that leads us to seek the highest. It may be the guiding light of morality and religious proscription that persuades us to counter our selfish desires with stronger, conflicting desires with a spiritual aim. But if able to succeed, our success would be a success of *will* ; in practice, the result could only be an increase in the very passions that have always insulated us from that highest which we seek.

It may be that spiritual guidance is "there" and available all the time. If so, it can only be the barrier of passions, our normal human desires, our nature, that prevents us receiving the benefits of this strange flow of awareness. Many have tried, but the harder one tries to break through the barrier of passions, the stronger it becomes, because to *try* is to use the will. To *try* means building an extra barrier of passion at the very point where the will needs to be broken. It becomes evident, sooner or later, that the opposite approach is required. Hindu sages of old realized that: "the sacrifice of thoughts and feelings opens a door to admit the spirit".

Anyone interested in astrology possesses a certain curiosity about themselves, in the deepest sense. There can be few characteristics more human than this. It is certainly a step in the right direction, for a step towards *ourselves* is a step towards truth. The reason why we want to know more about ourselves is probably because we sense the need for change within. Thoughtful people are forever applying some sort of personal analysis to themselves, even if only by filling in the questionnaire of popular psychology: which attitude is nearest your own, a, b, or c? It is all a response to this deep need. Particularly when religion has lost its grip, people will always seek a key that will unlock the inner self and allow the soul to develop.

Personal analysis is always interesting; but no amount of probing and tinkering within the mind can of itself lead to a change within the soul. The seeker may well acquire hidden knowledge and achieve unusual understanding, but the condition of the soul cannot be improved by trying, whether by thinking, or feeling, or physical exercise, through esoteric studies, or yoga, or religion, or hypnotism, or asceticism, or anything else. Not a few set out to modify those characteristics already built in at the moment of birth; but if they succeed they may complicate still further their already complicated personality. Unwanted characteristics, ignored or denied, will still be present in the soul whether or not they are acceptable in the context of religion, or morality, or even common sense. Deeply seated turmoil may result, and this can produce unrealistic attitudes, or depression, or even mental illness.

In some parts of the world, particularly in the East, when people become aware of the harmful influences that seem to surround them on all sides, they may decide to withdraw from worldly affairs, to seek to atone, or to become a "holy person" by doggedly refusing to entertain or even to acknowledge all the desires of the world. But there is a certain risk involved in this type of practice. If it works — if a hermit seems to have succeeded in isolating himself spiritually, he may have created for himself a symbolic shell, an artificial cover for the soul. He may not be able to feel bad influences, but neither will he be able to receive good ones if they should appear. He will have become trapped, as it were, in the centre of his own personal mandala, the cocoon that ought to be nurturing a potentially perfect human being. His soul will have become smothered and rendered insensitive to any but the coarsest of influences. He may well have achieved unruffled tranquility, but it is not an enviable state. It may prove to be the meaningless tranquility of a corpse.

We cannot avoid the legacy symbolized by our own birth chart; we simply have to remain receptive and fully aware of everything that happens to us. A hypnotic state, a trance, whether self-induced or involuntary, can only be of negative value. Any new influence received in a less-than-conscious state is almost certain to be of less-than-human origin. The great majority of influences that reach us during life inevitably possess an origin below the truly human status. Whether we see worldly passions as unwanted instincts, zodiacal influences, or ethical dilemmas, it seems impossible to avoid them. The harder we struggle with them, the more firmly does their influence become ensconced within the inner feelings.

In any birthchart, the horoscope has to be a symbol of *becoming* within a creative cycle of life. Now, by applying astrology to a study of the inner self, our hope is to complete that cycle, to attain unity. Unity in this sense implies the atonement, the coming together of separated parts, that may lead to escape from what Hindus call the "web of illusion". The web of illusion, in our terms, is no more nor less than the zodiac itself. The cycle of the horoscope; the cycle of the self; physical, psychological, "spiritual" cycles; we may perceive "cycles of becoming" according to our own contents, our own aspirations. Certainly there is the type of cycle which, completed within the limits of time, may lead to rebirth and a new self on the level of personality. But our ambition is now set on a higher cycle which, continued as a spiral in space, leads on to ever-expanding growth, towards eventual oneness with the source.

Like the goddess Kali, the passions are at the same time life sustainers and life destroyers. The material life forces are the coarsest and most powerful of all the zodiacal influences that assail us, and yet our bodies, brains and hearts, are themselves material objects. Our thinking, as a product of that materiality, cannot reasonably be relied upon to find a way of evading the material forces that govern our lives. It is a real problem, and not merely a game of snakes and ladders using the symbols of astrology. We are caught up in a web of powerful forces working at a deep level, and unless these natural forces can be stilled, or diverted, or made inoperative in some way, out situation seems likely to remain unaltered.

Centuries ago, perhaps, a way out could be found merely by following the teachings of great religious founders. Devout followers may still be convinced that faith, or even simple belief, is all that is required. Many others, however, have grown sceptical over the years. A surge of belief, an emotional change of heart, is not the same as a spiritual change of content and soul-direction, for these things themselves belong to the desires — passions that grow ever stronger as hearts and minds over generations acquire greater capacity to feel and think. Probably, passions are stronger now than they were in less sophisticated centuries; there are certainly far more "influences" about. Certainly, there were far fewer distractions.

Whatever point of view we take, it seems plain that we need to reverse the existing trend, to avoid being overlaid completely by the coarser influences of nature working through the complexities of our civilization. We need, I am sure, to prepare ourselves in some way so that we are ready to receive such finer influences as may filter in to our sphere from beyond the zodiac. And I am sure too that the only way for this to be achieved is by somehow stilling the flow of influences, the everyday desires that normally fill our hearts and minds. The principle is straightforward enough. How, though, can it be put into practice?

It goes against the grain of education, of everything we have learnt, to suggest that keen thinking and deep feeling about some goal may makes its attainment less, rather than more likely. We have always been taught that we should concentrate our minds with determination, and feel what is to be felt with sincerity. But such exhortations as these work only *within* the sphere of the

210

Zodiac; within the realm of materiality and the clutches of the goddess Kali. Ethical values are essential for civilization, but they can create barriers within the self, forming a protective armour of prejudices and preconceptions. Moral ethics and religious principles form useful yardsticks of behaviour if we are to maintain a tolerable society, but even they may serve a negative purpose by cutting off diversified individuals from their own true nature. Virtuous living is concerned with outward behaviour, and takes no account of the soul and its contents.

For all who have commenced the second cycle of the three, the true calling of the soul is to be the leader of the individual. Wholeness cannot otherwise be accomplished. But as we may all discover sooner or later, all outside influences, all physical, emotional, and mental experiences find their way into the soul, and not merely the ethical or virtuous qualities. As the reception-centre for all influences, both high and low, it is the awakened soul alone that offers the means of escape from the enmeshing zodiac. In forming a smooth trine with Saturn, Jupiter may hold the key, and although a septile aspect with Pluto may synchronize with death, it will be the death of outward passions alone. But for this death to be meaningful these passions must first be accepted as one's own. To deny them is to deny the soul, and acceptance of the soul is the only means whereby mortals are able to contact spirit.

The human mansion

An ancient allegory describes human beings as like a great house with no master, and no steward in charge. There are numerous servants and staff, but few of them seem to be doing the job for which they were trained and employed; they behave as they please. The place is unkempt, full of squatters and unwanted guests, and frequently raided by thieves. The master himself is probably away somewhere; nobody knows or much cares. The legitimate steward — the human soul — has been held prisoner in the cellar by rebellious servants all these years. Once released, he could pick up the telephone and ask the real master — spirit — to come and put

ASTROLOGY AND THE INNER SELF

his house in order. When the master arrives he will oust any unwanted lodgers and fit anti-burglar devices. But he will sack none of the servants, however unruly they may have been; when his benign influence is felt, all the staff will be glad to do their proper work.

Some systems of work on the self, such as Gurdjieff's "Fourth Way", are aimed at creating an inner "self", a super-ego who could be put in charge of this house. He is not meant to be master, or even the legitimate steward, but merely "deputy steward", in charge until the situation improves. There is a distinct disadvantage to this self-help system, assuming its successful completion: one will have created something extra in oneself that should not really be there. Once the real steward — the human soul — has been discovered and reinstated, and the master — spirit — has paid his long-awaited visit, the self-created deputy steward, the artificial "self", will have to go. In astrological terms, we might say, Jupiter and Neptune conjoined will oppose Mars. But after the mental and emotional concentration of effort involved in his creation, deputy steward will not want to go. He will probably not agree to be ruled by the real steward, and his forcible expulsion can be a problem. It is virtually impossible, by oneself, to remove something that has become interwoven into the tapestry of the inner feelings.

The inner feelings will have enough problems of their own without extra, artificial introductions.. This emotional compartment of the inner self normally contains many inherited features or characteristics inadvertently introduced, as it were, by the parents — if not at the time of conception then later on, during childhood. Characteristics of this hidden nature may not be traceable on the birth chart, but they are there nevertheless. When the steward is released, when the soul is roused from the stupor which has overcome it, the emotional field of the inner self is the area in which spiritual purification will spontaneously commence, once contact with the master of the house — an influx of spirit — has been made.

The concept of "Holy Spirit" is perhaps too well known to require astrological symbolism. Though non-material, it is no mere concept of words, as numerous people can attest. It is reality, whatever mental imagery such people may apply — a life-giving spark to be received. As we must all realize by now, spirit cannot be gained or received merely by wishing it. The Hindu Upanishads expressed it in succinct terms: "Spirit is not to be gained by wishing or choosing: spirit chooses". Once this non-personal choice has been made, however, the individual will be in no doubt about the fact. Purely on a psychological level, to a greater or lesser degree, the "collective experiences" of the human race, images of ancient mysteries and forgotten civilizations may flood in to bemuse the mind. Pluto and Uranus conjoined will oppose the retrograde Saturn.

The process of personal assimilation, the spiral towards completion, may have begun with a sense of uniqueness, of differentiation. But once under way it has to involve the further assimilation of everything previously conceived of as "collective", a coming to awareness of previously unsuspected soul-contents. The unconscious mind formulated by Jung as the common background from which individual consciousness arises was to be met with, he said, through symbolism. But when the movement towards wholeness has begun, this underlying current takes on a solid and perceptible form. Jung's process of individuation involves assimilation of unconscious contents by the conscious mind. But the sphere of the unconscious is vastly greater than that of the conscious, as the orbits of the outer planets symbolically show. A kind of possession by collective archetypes, self-aggrandizement, or what Jung called inflation, can result from mistaking these collective contents for one's own, and an attitude of submissive humility is essential.

On the spiritual journey too, one is merely a bystander, a member of the audience rather than an actor. What then is the difference between the process of psychological individuation on the one hand, and a spiritual journey of return to the source, on the other? Using the symbolism of astrology, both may be symbolized by integration with the Sun. But in the former case the inner self remains unchanged; only the personality develops and changes, surrounding the soul like a rich but smothering tapestry. Saturn, you could say, has conjoined with Mars. In the latter case the personality becomes lighter, thinner — threadbare, even. Jupiter now will have conjoined with Mars, and Saturn runs retrograde. There will be nothing to prevent divine influences entering the soul.

A channel for spirit

Many wise and pious people say that spirit is already present in the innermost being, working from the inside; others equally wise may visualize spirit as an extraneous force, visiting at will and working from the outside. Some of course will insist that "it is all in the mind". All these explanations, I suppose, are equally valid; whether divine visitor or hidden component of the self, there is no material reference on which we can call. As the Hindu Vedas put it: "spirit moves intimately through the things of this world, yet he is above these things".

People nowadays tend to be heavily material, both in their soul-contents and in their aspirations. New creativity of thought, coupled with untrammelled lightness of feeling, must have led sages of old to aspire to a wholeness of self beyond time. Modern minds swollen and overflowing with a surplus store of information become bound by time; our logical, analytical way of thinking falls inevitably under the sway of Saturn. The passions symbolized by Mars, drawing their strength from the life force of the zodiac, seem to clutch the Earth as closely as its atmosphere. If higher influences really do exist, can they break the spell and release the soul-steward from his prison — and if so, how are they to be contacted?

Perhaps all spiritual ideas tend to be naive, artless as they must be. Suppose we assume that such a contact must emerge from somewhere "up there". Surely, it must filter through the outermost,

214

rarified layers of the collective unconscious that surrounds us all. Planet-watchers have speculated about the strange wandering red spot of Jupiter, a perpetual disturbance in its atmosphere, its centre the eye of a great hurricane, the astrological eye of the soul. How can we symbolize the ingress or the egress, of spirit? Larger than the other planets put together, yet with a density only a quarter that of Earth, the enigmatic Jupiter is as shrouded by heavy cloud as the human soul is shrouded by layers of passion — by the very action of planetary evolution. Could a creative trine with Pluto signal the awakening, or could it be rather the septile aspect of death — the death of personal desire?

Do we need to find a way through the zodiac — through that seemingly unbroken skin of instinctual forces? It can be of no use to search for a particularly permeable degree as a spiritual stepping-off point from the personal cycle of becoming; or, as no one type of person is more "spiritual" than any other, to approach any particular type of personality. Rather, we have to assume that the weakest or most permeable point of the zodiac is at its centre — the symbolic centre of self, and the great cross of time within space. Because this central point is common to all, a focus for all influences, if one individual becomes able to receive higher influences, it follows that anyone else who is close to that person within space and time, if they are sufficiently receptive, will also experience a loosening of the barrier — a misty thinning of the structure of the zodiac within their own central point; a weakening of their own passions, to create their own channel for divine influence.

To a newborn child, this channel is still open. It is only as the child begins to learn, as feeling and thinking begin to develop, that the channel becomes blocked. This is how human cleverness and sensitivity have brought about our spiritual undoing. At birth, the channel is open and clear. But it soon becomes neglected and unused amid the profusion of new impressions, in effect covered over with ever-increasing layers of materiality until, after only a few years, the channel and the soul itself lie forgotten, their possibilities unsuspected by the fast-developing brain, too young at the time to remember. The contact was lost to humanity when innocent simplicity was lost. Innocent simplicity, very obviously, is not a characteristic of modern people. In any community the keenness of one's brain is a most valuable asset. Obviously one needs to apply a modicum of thought even to embark upon some kind of spiritual journey; and presumably one needs a certain emotional content too, in order to accept the idea as having value, and to determine actually to follow it.

The soul then needs to be stirred, to be resuscitated. But we have to remember the position of our soul-symbol Jupiter, midway between our passion-symbol Mars, and our death-symbol Saturn. Certain types of religious teaching can be misleading. When heard for the first time by the thinking brain, the voice of the soul may seem profane, or unethical, or irreligious, because it constitutes our own inner contents, and any or all of these may be expressed. But only this inner voice, however impure it may at first seem, can lead to the possibility of wholeness.

Occult practices at this time can be positively dangerous. Occult experiences imply an awareness of soul taking place before it has been properly awakened with spirit, when the red-eyed Jupiter is in conjunction with Mars, leading to strange and passionate experiences with the feelings. The occult can be addictive, and it is by no means to be confused with the spiritual. Bereft as it is of spirit, the occult offers no hope of escape from the karmic Wheel of Becoming, because the world of karma is its natural home. Like Eden's tempting serpent, more subtle than any beast of the field, the occult is wholly contained within the sphere of materiality. Despite its subtle nature, the occult is directly accessible from materiality, and still under the sway of the coarse influences that we have been trying to tame. At this stage we are still members of the audience and not the performers; we can experience and comment, but we cannot make things happen. Quite simply, if we try to produce non-material results in ourselves, if our will has taken part, such results will belong to the occult, the abstract dimension of materiality.

Creating gold from the elements

In alchemy, before the search became chemically orientated, the elusive philosophers' stone represented the hoped-for means to bring about a symbolic combination of the four mystical elements: fire — or, in our zodiac symbolism, the instinctual human element; air — the symbolic animal element; water — the instinctual plant element; and earth — the symbolic mineral or material element. All will indeed combine to create gold, but of course these are symbolic elements, and the gold also is allegorical. The four elements represent four basic passions of the human soul. We can say they represent four "lower souls", which by their union alone can allow the immortal fifth, the *rochani* self, to appear. In practice it entails a simultaneous harmonic expression of the four passions — observing, desiring, defending, acquiring — to produce their fusion. This combined passion is *compassion*, and the union initiates the mystical quality of spiritual love.

We might wish to visualize the creation of this immortal golden fifth passion by recalling the "mutable" quality of each elemental division of the zodiac at its "highest point". At this metaphorical point in each case the three quadruplicities — mutable, fixed and cardinal — can interact with the four triplicities of zodiac-quality — the kingdoms of nature: human, animal, plant and mineral — each combining with the life qualities of the division above it, finally to produce a completed quintile polygram. This is the upright five-pointed star symbolizing the completion of selfhood.

With each merger of separate elemental kingdoms, the septile aspect will be involved as the catalyst to be found between these "seven heavens", between barriers that are normally insurmountable. On Earth these are the barriers set up by nature to isolate the mineral world from that of the plants, the plant kingdom from that of the animals, the animal kingdom from the world of humans, and the human world from the higher worlds of sainthood and the *rochani* realms of spirituality. This is why the septile aspect is the aspect of death; it symbolizes the temporary passion-death which alone can enable the mutable third in every case to combine with the cardinal third of the natural division above it. It charts each metaphorical step to be taken, each spiritual hurdle to be surmounted.

From the macrocosm of the world of nature we can focus on the microcosm of the individual human soul. We see by the cycle of houses how each sign, each degree, with all the zodiac qualities, are potentially present within every individual from the moment of birth. From the birthpoint of entry within the first cycle the signs are traversed in a sequence of twenty-eight months each; each separate primary psychological function completes its rulership in eighty-four months; each full cycle of selfhood takes place over twenty-eight years, and one completed threefold lifespan lasts for eighty-four years.

By the mutable factor of zodiac quality, by the part of each one of us that corresponds in nature to the adaptability of Gemini, Virgo, Sagittarius and Pisces (the go-between in each case linking the fixed with the cardinal), steps can be taken up the metaphorical Jacob's ladder to the spiritual source. But as we have seen, steps in this direction cannot be initiated by the will, cannot be undertaken merely by wishing. Through concentrating, desiring, striving, grasping, the passions remain separate, and the elemental kingdoms remain isolated. We must accept that some kind of spiritual "contact" is necessary for the process to be initiated.

Zen masters say: "When spring comes, the grass grows by itself". Something must be allowed to happen, to reopen the closed channel of the soul. In practical terms, the person to be "opened" in this manner will stand close to another person who has already been "opened", and offer a willing "sacrifice of thoughts and feelings", relaxed but receptive in body and mind. Spirit will do the rest. Neither planets nor degrees, any more than thoughts or feelings, can play any active part in initiating the spiral of ascent, though all these things will certainly record the event and its deep significance.

"Soul" is not the same as "heart". As a romantic entity with real awareness of its own, the human heart likes to identify itself with the "poetic soul", and loves to feel that it alone possesses psychic awareness. The heart may believe that it actually *is* soul, or even the Holy Spirit. The heart can sometimes find it hard to bear, during the opening and awakening of the real soul, that it can do no more than bear witness to feelings more meaningful than its own, transmitted by some organ more subtle than itself. At such a time the heart may feel jealousy and fear. This is one good reason why the heart needs a traditional religion on which to rely.

Strange experiences

Practical experience is more convincing than theory. People who find themselves consciously experiencing their own soul for the first time will certainly become aware that something miraculous and deeply spiritual is happening. Many at this time will experience charismatic tongues and involuntary movements, but these experiences are by the way. Though they may be called "spiritual" they cannot be thought of as of value in themselves. They constitute a "throwing out" of unwanted soul contents, a neutralizing of everything within the self that has come about through use of the disunited passions.

The truth is that this personal soul, when it comes to consciousness, is not yet immortal. This personal soul, which soon becomes able to walk free of the body and report back to the senses, to hold conversations with the mind, to peer over tall buildings and distant horizons, to see into the future — even this non-material manifestation of the physical human body also lives within the laws of time and death. The personal soul-symbol Jupiter is still "mortal", still within the orbit of Saturn, and unless this miraculous soul has indeed been graced by receiving influences from beyond the collective soul-symbol Neptune, and thus acquired immortality, the limiting principle of Saturn will prevail.

Astrology represents the life-principle by the symbol of the Sun, centre of all orbits though free from their influence, radiant centre-point of the zodiac through which, symbolically, the spirit may enter. Spirit, at all events, is the only go-between, spanning the gulf and surmounting the barrier between the four divided realms under satanic rule, and the united wholeness of God. The ingress of spirit initiates the purification of soul contents. The process can only be involuntary, without involving desires, and we need to avoid fantasizing. Purification itself is wholly individual, and may seem foul or sweet, holy or profane. We should take no notice of the experiences of others: a sensible person can listen and judge, but should believe only the personal experience. Anything that arrives or is received in less than full consciousness, without full awareness, will have a source that is below the truly human level — a temptation, perhaps, of Satan, of the Earth. (As the biblical Book of Job points out, Satan is also a son of God, a member of the court of heaven, whose job it is to range over the Earth, governor of all material life-forms). The horizon of the mind aligned with the inner self crosses the centre of the mandala chart. Below that line is the unconscious sub-human world; above it, super-human awareness.

When the separate passions come to rest, even momentarily, suspended as it were in silent witness, at that point all human life is shared. We begin to become one, and this is indeed the common experience of those whose soul has been awakened by spirit. They are able to witness the soul-contents of each, for "when consciousness enters the heart, the feelings of others become known". This can be a strange experience, an intercourse of souls, which has often but quite erroneously been described as "thought transference". When a person attains some degree of wholeness, he or she begins to perceive others as wholes rather than a collection of parts. Intuitively, such people can grasp the whole nature of another person or circumstance, as it applies personally there and then. In effect, they have gained an insight into the nature of each moment.

The thinking mind, with the intuitive faculty, the feelings and sensations; the more these can unite in sensing the meaning of the moment, the more balanced will we be and the less will we be bound by materiality. The smallest movement towards the creation of wholeness is an act of attunement which will lead ultimately to atonement. Those who have begun to be whole, whose souls have come to awareness, live in a world of whole meanings. But it is only the light of spirit that will enable the soul to operate as a fully conscious entity. Without that light, it can be no more than an insubstantial shadow, a primordial image; something to be glimpsed darkly in dreams.

While the passions are suspended, a person's innermost contents are being cleaned out, as it were, and renewed stage by stage, in an extended journey towards wholeness. And unlike a cloistered monk or a lone yogi, or a member of some religious commune, such people are able to devote their full normal attention to their worldly affairs, without affecting their spiritual progress. They can rest secure in the knowledge that the inner self is free to grow and climb unimpeded.

So a cleaning-out process is essential, and it can begin only through quiet submission to higher influences. And the channel of receiving will be clearest when in the presence of others who have already received the contact. The physical body, used to working under control of the senses, the feelings and the thoughts, should experience for itself a type of movement quite independent of the usual stimuli, quite innocent of will. The mouth may speak by inward volition, without prompting, often raising matters which were previously unknown and often, indeed, to be thought unknowable. The source of such phenomena is beyond the power of will, and outside the scope of learning.

The nose may experience smells that have no material origin. The mind, silently witnessing, will understand something about the origins of incense, and feel the atmosphere of peaceful devotion that accompanies it. The ears may hear and interpret words that have no equivalent in language. The eyes may see events before they occur, or be shown things hidden from physical sight. When the curious brain decides to investigate, or when the feelings can no longer resist the desire to participate, such phenomena disappear, for they cannot be desired, willed or enjoined. Trying to understand, the brain has to acknowledge that the one expressing these physical movements, smells, sights and sounds, is a subtle body able to come to life only when thoughts and emotions are inactive; a subtle body — the soul — that seems to gain vigour through exercise. It is an after-death experience, happening during life.

Once opened in this way, the soul should remain open. The moving spirit may seem to be present or not. It is an ongoing process of purification and not an entertainment, and one's personal preferences should play no part. The experience should not be taken for granted, neither should it be sought out. Pride no longer has a legitimate place in the psyche. The ancient words of the Upanishads will now make new sense: "He who smells ethereal incense is only in the valley plain. He who hears ethereal voices is only approaching the foothills. He who see ethereal visions is only nearing the foot of the mountain. The pure mountain air is free of perfume, voices, and visions".

CHAPTER 9

The spiral of ascent

From the ascendant on the birth chart the point of self traverses by degrees the whole cycle of the zodiac, experiencing the abstract quality of nature symbolized by it. As it travels it acquires less-than-human characteristics, steadily gaining material strength but leaving far behind the initial contact of the newly born with the spiritual source. So having made what amounts to a quite involuntary descent amongst what we can now identify as increasingly coarse influences, through the instinctual worlds of humans, then animals, then plants, and then material objects, having as an adult person experienced their varied natures, there comes a time to gather these elements personally within the self, and begin the return journey. Now that we have become aware of the situation, we are in a position to put theory into practice, to put our own house in order. From this point on, besides our normal everyday pursuits, a submissive completion of wholeness should be a major aim in life.

The birth chart native's symbolic Sun needs to have been reached before this return journey can be made; but what does this mean in practical terms? The vague concept of a "redeeming spirit" has to come to reality; actual contact with spirit is a necessary precursor for the final path of the soul. This is the allegorical house-master come home, with authority to reinstate the steward and allow him to carry out his proper duties. Without real spiritual contact, without the channelling process and corresponding inner development, the abstract sphere of collective humanity will remain a nebulous world of dreams, a land of the unconscious. This is where a truly practical while at the same time submissive and unwilled method needs to be found.

Imagine the fate of a soul only partially "opened", perhaps by occult practices. By its own nature, it will receive contents and adopt them, believing them to be its own. Still bound by the abstract zodiac of materiality, such a soul trapped without spirit in collective realms is fated to remain tied to Earth after the death of the body. Existence on Earth without the physical principle of Saturn to give materiality or substance to individual passions, could only be a living death, abortive and empty. It might bring to mind Milton's *Paradise Lost:*

> *As far removed from God and light of heav'n*
> *As from the centre thrice to th'utmost pole.*

Pluto will have taken charge. As the governing symbol of collective mortality, Pluto is also the ancient god of ghosts, keeper of the dark underworld of the unconscious, far from the light and warmth of the Sun.

It really does seem that deliberately overruling or suppressing your own personality and concentrating on the abstract side of your nature, a purely selfish, occult cultivation of the soul without leaving room for spirit, can lead to a ghost-like state after death. Within Buddhism, personality is sometimes decried and often denied; the everyday material world of *samsara* is considered illusory, and much store is set on the meditation of *samadhi* to attain the cessation of passions, hoping eventually to reach the ultimate stillness of *Nirvana.* But, as hinted at in some of the ancient Buddhist "wisdom poems", all is not quite what it seems. The apparent peace of *Nirvana* may itself be contained within those deceptive passions, the calm eye of the hurricane:

In the Buddhist view the cycle of common humanity, with the inevitability of death within the laws of nature, may well result in rebirth in one form or another. And the same philosophical theme teaches that some individuals may lose the thread of humanity altogether by cutting themselves off, as it were, from the light of their own Sun. By this understanding, at death, instead of completing the "natural" zodiac-bound cycle of human-to-human reincarnation, they may become absorbed instead by whatever life forces have formed their inner centre of gravity. If their own nature has been unduly sympathetic, or antipathetic, towards these instinctual forces and the beings they govern, their soul may be drawn involuntarily into progressively more solid worlds of animals, plants, or even material objects, to experience who-knows-what future "lives" within these states.

Aspects of heaven

There are many varied traditions of heaven, hell, or after-life abodes of the soul, and any or all of these intuitively perceived states may exist as subtle realities. There are said to be sensual heavens, heavens of desire, each a material paradise of the passions at some symbolic point between Earth and Sun. These involve inner states wherein the soul may continue to enjoy food and drink, be waited upon by ephemeral beings of voluptuous beauty, eager to further gratify the senses; places where shady trees, cool fountains, luscious fruits, flowers and jewels abound. If such "lower heavens" can be pictured as existing beyond the self, they will necessarily be confined within the orbit of Saturn. The soul which has earned a sensual paradise may enjoy it for a brief while. But such a situation depends on the continuation of personal desires after death, still within the bounds of time; it too must come to an end along with those desires. Such a soul still belongs to Earth, and being drawn towards earthly desires, to Earth it will return when the time comes for renewal.

Any psychological or religious system worth its salt aims towards creating an eventual oneness; and if any of them are pursued thoroughly, they may well achieve this aim. Personal results may seem worthwhile, even saintly; they may seem to be "working", but having arisen through strength of will they are unlikely to result in spiritual development. The point is, spirit cannot be willed, and a heaven without spirit is likely to prove transitory, a paradise that will eventually lead back to a renewed cycle of earthly becoming. The biblical king Solomon with his wisdom and wealth epitomized humanity at the peak of material light-power, as one who had climbed by an interior route to reach the translucent but impenetrable roof of instinctual materiality. A temporary paradise without spirit could well be said to represent the "temple of Solomon". It has often been said that one person's heaven may be another's hell. The satanic forces and the life forces of materiality are but different names for the same thing.

The planetary aspects detailed in chapter six can now be seen to take more meaningful form. The quintile aspects apply wholly to the individual. They symbolize the points of transition between major centres of gravity, between the qualities of different passions as perceived by the developing soul of a child. The descending point of self finds its own level, its own sticking point. The septile aspects, on the other hand, apply to the progress or ascent of an individual within the cosmos. They symbolize the points of transition from one major division of zodiacal instincts to the next, the stepping-off point between mineral and plant, between plant and animal, animal and human. They represent the journey of a rising or transcendent point of self.

This diagram opposite, showing the septile aspects, forms a universal mandala: a symbol of the evolutionary process of the world. Above the horizon is the source of spiritual influence. Below the horizon is ordinary life as we all know it, under the laws of nature. The point of self, the soul, traversing or imbibing instinctual human life forces concentrated along the eastern (left) horizon near the birth ascendant, begins to shed the spiritual consciousness of the newly born as it leaves the *rochani* level of "higher humans" or saints. On the western (right) horizon of the descendant, the material, or mineral, or satanic life forces become open again to spiritual awareness as they approach their highest (and simultaneously, paradoxically, their lowest) level, close to the *rabbani* level of archangels. The descendant now is an archangelic descendant, the allegorical fall of the Archangel Lucifer, the point where heavenly light falls into the zone of materiality.

Light of Wisdom
"Integrity of the newborn child"
Spiritual enlightenment

Light of Science
"Fall of the Archangel Lucifer"
Occult enlightenment

ANGELIC

SAINTLY

ARCHANGELIC

HUMAN

MATERIAL

ANIMAL

PLANT

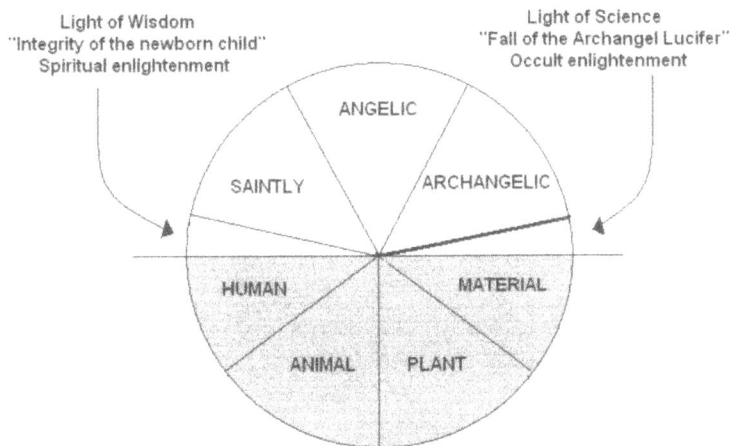

The Septile Aspects: a Universal Mandala

It need come as no surprise to be reminded how close is the archangelic to the satanic. The illuminated space within which the light of wisdom descends does indeed represent the temple of Solomon. It is the place of material, sensual heavens. It is the same euphoric state as that said to be experienced, albeit briefly, by people subjected to super G-forces; the same as those whose near-death experiences give them a glimpse of the Elysian Fields. It is from this, the very lowest abstract point of the material division — apparently deep within the satanic realm — that a person may acquire marvellous knowledge. It may be scientific knowledge, or religious knowledge; or supernatural powers. It may even be the wisdom of Solomon: there is nothing "bad" about it. It is a place of miracles, but it is not the realm of the Holy Spirit. There is "a great gulf fixed" beyond which the human soul cannot travel in that direction.

Astrological pilgrim

In outer space there is no real rising or falling: both are the same. Similarly in inner space one may *seem* to be ascending whilst actually being drawn lower by the forces of material gravity. To sink deeper in spiritual terms can seem, in terms of worldly ambition, like climbing higher. When a newborn baby begins to learn and become less babylike as worldly influences encroach, dimming what we can now understand as the saintly light of closeness to the source, those subtle inner feelings become swamped until, by the time a child's mental powers have developed and the emotions are fully functioning, this inborn source of guidance is completely overshadowed. Of course it is good, and essential in any civilized society, to be able to experience to the full the world of things; but from the point of view of the soul it seems unfortunate. By the age of puberty, the individual will have sunk in spiritual terms from the original human level to the psychic level of materiality, and there the majority stay.

Adult people, with few exceptions, are psychically centred somewhere within the material septile zone, beneath the horizon of awareness. The wonderful zone of light is not far away, above our heads. Initial contact with spirit may nudge us gently into this zone to experience minor miracles for ourselves, a foretaste of spiritual awareness; but we will soon come to the understanding that this is not where we are to remain. This is not "heaven". It is an inferior "paradise". This place represents the highest point attainable directly from the material zone, and there is no through route to the spiritual worlds beyond; no way accessible from the side of the descendant. If we are to climb during this lifetime towards spiritual worlds, it has to be by way of the vegetable, the animal, and eventually the human levels, discarding by degrees those instinctual characteristics acquired on the way down — those characteristics that are more appropriate for the well-being of plants and animals than of humans.

When on receiving a divine spark, a person begins to make

228

progress through the septile divisions towards the human level, a sense of loss may accompany that progress. Such a one may suffer the disappointment of seeming to lose their sense of the miraculous; they may even, perhaps, feel abandoned by wisdom. Like John Bunyan they will feel that they have become pilgrims through a barren land. There is little enlightenment and precious few material rewards to be gleaned within the dull realms of the plants and the animals. A dark and barren course it may be; but only by allowing our souls to retrack in this way can we "become again like little children" in the Christian sense, and reapproach our own higher selves and the possibility of wholeness.

As this spiritual journey gets under way, though we may seem to have lost contact with the miraculous events that preceded it, as our viewpoint changes we can begin to understand and appreciate all the various religious teachings that have left us untouched previously. But this is not a path known to religious leaders of today, nor is it the ascetic's path of moral discipline; neither is it the callous chain of consequences within plant and animal life, as dictated by nature. This is the path of inner guidance, and all who follow it can be assured that their own inner self will guide them in the manner best suited to their individual needs. No-one else can now lead or direct. It is not something with which others need agree or disagree, approve or disapprove, praise or censure. None can stand between a pilgrim and God.

We can see now why the septile aspects of death are to be identified with the major divisions of cosmic life forces. During the course of our lives everything we have known, and more besides, has sunk into our innermost feelings, and in the normal course of events nothing of this can be taken away until we face eventual death. As a rule, therefore, any improvement in the status of our soul would have to depend on, or follow from, our own physical death. Saturn must have his way. But now, with spiritual contact, having touched our own Sun, it is not the soul itself but only the *contents* of the soul that must die, or seem to die, again and again if need be, as each septile aspect is reached and passed by the point of Self.

Looked at from the outside, an overall pattern may be emerging as you, the astrological pilgrim, begin this great spiral of ascent. Obviously enough, the "spiritual" level of materiality corresponds with the actual source of all material attainments useful to civilization. Whilst retraversing this division in the course of ascent, whatever you have been good at in the past you will be good at now — or probably better. Often, at this stage, outsiders might observe that you have indeed become in some way "spiritual": it is a time for strange phenomena. Later, when climbing through the tangled plant levels of being, miraculous happenings will dwindle; but, as though to compensate, your emotional awareness will be correspondingly heightened, your energy intense. Typically, though you may be at your most confident and energetic, you will seem to have lost contact with the means to make and hold on to money. The time will have come to "consider the lilies of the field" and have faith that the lord will provide — your own soul will be in charge of your welfare.

Later still, passing through the animal level of spiritual content, your brains will seem to be functioning in a more creative way than previously. Spiritual experiences may seem to be a thing of the past, but your imaginative, creative inspirations will excel. Then as you reach the beginnings of the human level, your intellectual prowess may seem to weaken, your brain may seem to falter and function on half-power; but to make up for this dullness your intuitive capacity will have increased. At this time you may seem oddly vulnerable, subject to criticisms and assaults, real or imaginary. But this difficult phase will pass as you receive finer influences directly from the intuitive centre of your psyche. This may prove an especially good time for artistic endeavour, for the kind of creative work, perhaps, that does not require keen supervision by the brain. But this phase too will pass, and you will find that you are now using all your faculties together, with increasing effect.

This sequence, of course, will vary greatly in detail and impact from person to person. But its ups and downs may cause family, friends and acquaintances to conclude that you have lost the once-keen edge of your mind, and this is because you, the astrological pilgrim, will have ceased to analyse critically. Perhaps for the first time you will be perceiving wholenesses wherever you look, and you will no longer be interested in separating and analyzing parts. All of your own past experiences will have become incorporated into this ever-increasing state of wholeness of being; everything is beginning to work in harmony.

Retrospectively perhaps, few of these ascending perceptions will have had the flavour of "spirituality" , as do those experiences many people meet with when their souls are first opened within the material, occult zone. You will have been obliged to experience, as it were, the dull repetitiveness of plant life; the instinctively predictable and unadventurous passions of the animal world; the intellectual emptiness of primitive, unschooled humanity. All this had to happen as your own inner feelings were being exposed and shaken out. In effect, you have had to undergo the repeated death of soul-contents, and at every hurdle you may with justification have felt that something precious has been lost. But any such sense of loss is only temporary. The value: the lessons and experiences of the past, are all still there, within the inner self. They are merely in the process of combining, whilst the transcendent human passion is being formed from separate material, plant, animal and ordinary-human elements: the earth, the water, the air, the fire. All will be returned to awareness, correctly channelled, once you have reached your high-human point of ascendancy.

Elemental souls

To express the same principle in different terms: the strange succession of soul-content deaths experienced by those following this ascending course, can be looked at in a more individual way. Remember that the deaths take place on the level of the passions, the desires, only, and these passions can now be seen as lower souls, or separate aspects of the whole soul itself. Like members of a family within the individual, these lower souls are sometimes called "brothers", or "sisters". They are to be symbolized by the astrological elements, earth, water, air, and fire. All the soul-elements are present, even after the apparent death of one of them; but as a rule only one at a time can carry the centre of gravity and act as spokesperson. The individual's actions — your actions — will then be coloured by whichever soul-element, whichever passion, happens to be dominant at the time, depending on the situation in which you find yourself.

The "lowest" soul, soul-element of earth, manipulator of the material life forces, has been called "black brother". Magicians of old who practiced material, manipulatory magic, used to work on the development of this earth-soul, their own black brother, to such a degree that it is said he was able to take on a solidly tangible form, manipulate surrounding passions and attract material objects, especially money and valuables, to himself. When isolated in this way, the chief feature of this earth-soul is seen to be "greed". But it will also be seen that, when working in harmony with his "brothers" in a whole, spiritually inclined person, the sublimated quality of greed becomes the ability to acquire the essentials of life, assuring that you will always have enough for yourself and your dependants.

When standing alone as the occult slave of a real magician, the elemental earth-soul, with its most powerful of passions, represents the strength of materiality on the occult plane. When taking the place of compassion — the combined passions — as a quintile degree, the pentagram will point downwards towards the Earth itself, forming a pentacle. The outline of a pentacle is said to resemble the head and face of a billy-goat, with ears, horns and beard, and this occult creation is said to have a goat-like smell too.

I have mentioned the biblical Book of Job, which rationalizes the power of Satan in religious terms. It is this "black brother", this elemental earth-soul, that represents the human standpoint of the way in which "Satan" is able to function. As Job was to discover, one can only receive "the blessings of God" according to one's own nature: through one's own self, one's own natural set of instincts. The "temptations" of Job (at the beginning of an ascending spiral) were the exact opposite of the material temptations which we might expect to befall us today: they were brought about by the *withdrawal* of the satanic or material force; the *weakening* of Job's elemental earth-soul, resulting in his loss of health and wealth. There is a great deal of built-in contradiction in religious attitudes towards this "evil power" to which we are all subject. A person in whom Satan is not operative — cursed with a weak earth-soul — would have no possessions and no influence in the world. Remember the allegory of the great house and the unruly servants. Plainly, earth-soul makes a first-rate and most valuable servant, but a ruthlessly dangerous master.

Continuing the spiral of ascent: when the appropriate septile aspect is reached marking the symbolic boundary between elemental earth and elemental water, the nature of water and the abstract nature of plants can be seen as though translated into human terms: changeable fluidity; violent action contrasting with dormant inactivity. Ruthless suppression and submissive meekness; anger, intolerance and aggression, but also mild defensiveness and the desire to live harmoniously in peaceful beauty. The urge to reproduce unrestrainedly, ranged against the need for strict discrimination and specific boundaries. The tendency to tower menacingly, or to creep surreptitiously. All these are the contradictory qualities of plants, and no less of the water on which they depend. In human attitudes, all are to be seen in the characters of those people currently being ruled by their plant-soul, whilst the water element is playing a major role in their soul-life.

When plants are not actually dormant, they can display surprising strength and tenacity: a humble dandelion can force its way through paved road surfaces; quite small creeping plants can smother and kill their neighbours. While passing through this phase on an ascending spiral many people actually feel drawn towards plants in practical commercial terms or in some other way. It can be a time of great activity; like the plants themselves their energy can be phenomenal. But while the wealth-orientated earth-soul is itself dormant, any such enterprise is unlikely to prove a financial success.

By esoteric tradition, plant-soul in human form, like earth-soul, is ascribed a colour. This is "red brother", or "red sister". As the point of self progresses, this red soul too eventually comes to maturity, goes through its own personal phase of suffering through the loss of its own passionate contents, and apparently dies. There is a powerfully emotional quality attached to this lower soul, and as the time comes for a further change in the spiritual centre of gravity, another hurdle of the septile divisions, a person may feel emotionally drained. They may find they have lost the will to work — or even at times, the will to carry on living. But this loss of inner confidence is a purely temporary, transitional phase. Very soon a new member of their personal family is born and comes to awareness.

Perhaps there is less to be said about "air" as an elemental soul quality, than can be said about "water", though the contents of an animal-soul person will be that much more varied and broadly based than those of the plant-soul body which preceded it. Such people are, of course, that much closer to the human norm than are the Earth-bound needs of the plant world. The name traditionally given to the soul filled with and motivated by animal life forces is "yellow brother", or "yellow sister". Perhaps we could say that the characteristic passion of this animal-soul, or the air element expressed in human terms, is "freedom of desire". Certainly the life of an animal within nature is limited not so much by long-term ambition as by the needs of the moment. In animal terms, the needs of the moment are usually connected either with food or with sexual relations. But animal patterns of social and sexual behaviour are more orderly, more temperate and less variable than the indiscriminate pollination and seeding, and jostling for place, that are typical of the plant world. Animals do tend to breed and order their social lives according to strict patterns and seasons, and

234

they are usually unquestioningly faithful to their own inherited social structure.

By the same measure, animal-soul people normally follow a reasonably conventional life, seldom giving offence to the prevailing code of moral behaviour. But more important from our present viewpoint is the fact that animals, and animal-soul people, are to a large extent free agents, having become, as it were, unplugged from the Earth. The arrival of this "yellow soul", and the strengthening of the elemental animal nature as the centre of psychic gravity, means that the ascending personality is able to exercise a higher degree of free will in making moral decisions. Plant-soul people, logically, are still governed largely from "below", and even whilst following the guidance of their own awakened soul, their lives will continue to be coloured by accumulated karmic content. The transition from plant-soul to animal-soul involves a symbolic uprooting. Unlike plants, animals have a brain. As black brother received his life guidance into the coarse physical body, and red brother received his life guidance directly into the feelings, so yellow brother now receives life guidance directly into the brain — into the thoughts.

When the time comes, as the next septile division is reached, animal-soul will falter, and as it does so the thoughts may seem to have become bemused. But again the lapse is only temporary, whilst a new lower soul gains strength and takes control. This is "white brother" or "white sister": a soul filled primarily with the influence of the human life force, representing the allegorical element of fire, and the zodiacal force that we must assume was created originally for the guidance of human beings on Earth. The subject with a predominantly human-soul receives instinctual guidance directly into the seat of consciousness, and in some ways this is a state comparable to that of a newborn child. If the human-soul can be said to represent a passion, it is the passion of observation, of seeing to the subtle core of any matter — the vision of ancient seers.

The inner self needs to have lived through the whole sequence of lower souls in order to approach the possibility of wholeness. It is of no use to imagine that the combination of soul-elements is the same whether the individual is ascending or descending, or whether the centre of psychic gravity is "material" or "human". For these lower souls to assemble themselves with materiality to the fore is symbolically to invert the quintile pentagram, to create a pentacle of occult intent. Human reassembly at this stage of inner development really needs to be centred in human-soul — a symbolic return to our lost spiritual childhood. There, we can await a further septile aspect — the most significant hurdle of all — and the emergence of the *real* human soul: the combined *rochani* soul of the whole human being.

The whole person

The septile divisions themselves, of course, can only represent a simplification of elemental realities. Within each division there are bound to be numerous "sevens within sevens". Dane Rudhyar visualized this apparent confusion as the music of creation, culminating in the transformation of human nature, represented by patterns of musical scales — for of course a musical "octave" is actually a recurrent sequence of seven — interplaying, swelling and fading, sometimes simple, sometimes intricate, crossing and recrossing. The diagram which follows shows the familiar sequence of the "Lifespan of the Patriarch", but this time occupying the spiral of ascent, and representing an *upwards* movement.

Earth-soul will now occupy Pisces, Aquarius and Capricorn. The "unworldly impressionability" of mutable Pisces can now be identified as the light of spirituality able to shine in those nether regions of Earth — the darkly material approaches to the temple of Solomon — imparting an inkling of spiritual wisdom. Then follows the "unconventional progress" of Aquarius upwards towards the source, the "prudent discipline" of the cardinal Capricorn keeping the self on the right track.

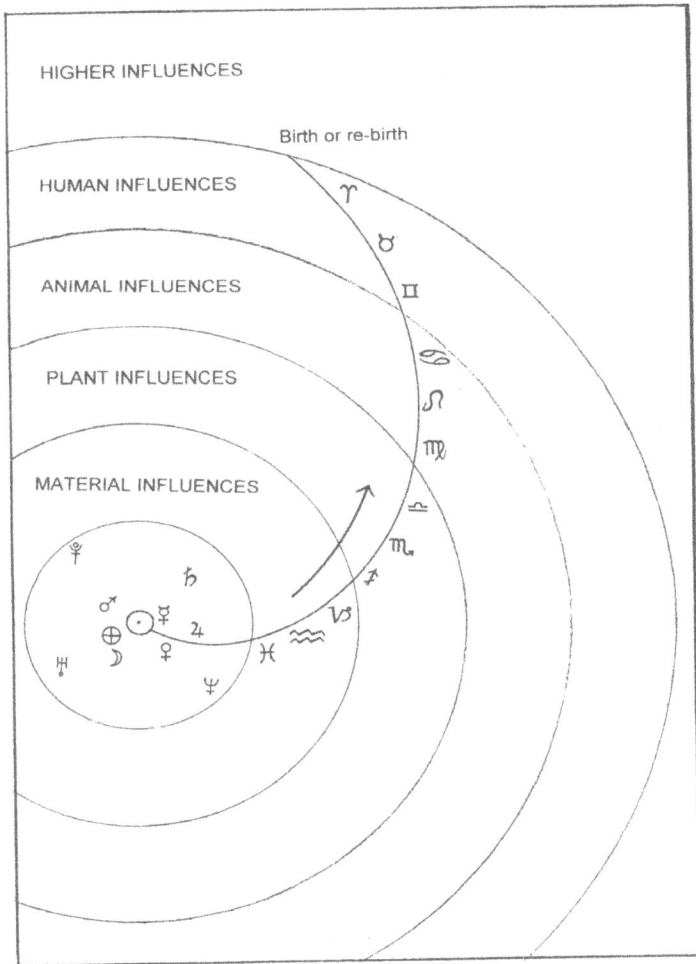

The Spiral of Ascent

Plant-soul now occupies Sagittarius, Scorpio and Libra. The "extensive exploration" of mutable Sagittarius is centred on the abstract nature of plants, deeply strengthened by the "intense penetration" of Scorpio. The "harmonious unity" of the cardinal Libra expresses the stability of a plant community at the peak of its development.

237

Animal-soul now occupies Virgo, Leo and Cancer. Free from the abstract roots which held the plants to Earth, mutable Virgo can now bring "critical analysis" to bear with a newly activated "animal" brain. The increasingly "authoritative power" of Leo is guarded by the "defensive protection" symbolized by the cardinal Cancer, building the defences that even the most advanced animals need when faced with the dangers of the world.

Human-soul now occupies Gemini, Taurus and Aries. With the newly acquired "adaptive variability" of mutable Gemini, with the truly "productive security" of Taurus, with intelligent construction taking the place of mere defence, we finally arrive at the cardinal Arien point of "urgent projection", aimed upwards and outwards, towards the possibility of new birth, new life.

With the first degree of Aries symbolically regained, a major cycle of transformation will be complete — the four lower souls can combine at last into one whole, higher soul. This saintly being has been called "brown brother" or "brown sister", a composite of the white, the yellow, the red, and the black, all restored to new life with new strength, united in power and purpose.

Once this amalgamation, this basic unity, has been achieved, each individual soul-family member, with their own unique qualities of persuasion, practicality, penetration, caution, daring, long-sightedness, judgment, and sensitivity, will be ready to step forward and take command as the need arises — with the support now of the whole family. Where material matters of profit and loss are foremost, earth-soul is truly able to cope. For situations needing expansive energy and aggression, plant-soul will come into its own. For clever brainwork and the regulation of desires, animal-soul can stand forward. And for any matters requiring "human" insight, careful observation and attention to detail, human-soul will be available with the necessary expertise.

The person whose psychic centre of gravity is the brown

rochani soul, is truly well balanced. Such a person, you may say, stands at a halfway stage within the universal hierarchy; he or she contains something of the nature of higher things, of influences that originate above the human condition, whilst still a physical person of the Earth. The distinctive passion corresponding with this united condition is the outcome of all other passions when they are felt simultaneously: compassion, an all-embracing love.

If Adam and Eve existed in fact, it is reasonable to suppose that they were a brown-skinned couple. From that original allegorical unity, a gradual scattering of humanity resulted in all the different races with their varying colours, passions and prejudices. It is one way of looking at that fabled descent, or eviction from the Garden of Eden. We can now see that a return to that original spiritual "brownness" takes us to the very roof of the Earth-bound passions; to the symbolic point beyond Pluto where our spiral of ascent bursts through the zodiac, leaving planets, symbols and fragmented passions far behind; to the point where we are helpless to do anything but submit blissfully to the will of God.

We have travelled some way from the birth chart horoscope. Synchronicity is our key; astrology need no longer stand apologetically, confronting the scorn of astronomy, uneasily on guard against the assaults of science. Their aims are totally different. The innate truth which astrologers have always sensed lies hidden within this ancient art, can emerge from the hinterland of part truths and dubious facts served up, as a rule, with just a hint of wishful thinking.

I hope that this book has shown that astrology, by way of *symbolic* truth, is maturing at last into one of the many gateways leading to spiritual reality.

INDEX

www.ingramcontent.com/pod-product-compliance
Lightning Source LLC
Chambersburg PA
CBHW060506090426
42735CB00011B/2123